why's

(*poignant*)

guide to Ruby

Tenderly written and illustrated by
why the lucky stiff

why's
(*poignant*)
guide to Ruby

Tenderly written and illustrated by
why the lucky stiff

This edition published 2020 by
Consonance, General Products Ltd https://consonance.app
for Brighton Ruby https://alt.brightonruby.com/

Foreword

Hello there, and welcome to your printed copy of the (poignant) guide to Ruby. This is either a joyful throwback to your early Ruby years, or a mystifying relic full of cartoon foxes and Ruby syntax. Possibly both.

This book was one of many projects bestowed upon us by Why the Lucky Stiff[1], a pseudonymous writer, cartoonist, artist and programmer, and one of the key figures in the early vanguard of the Ruby language outside Japan.

He left our community in 2009 and vanished, I like to think retiring to a mystic cave surrounded by humorous cartoon animals. I hope he's well and happy.

---

1 Publisher's note: although he is often referred to as "_why" or "_ why the lucky stiff" on the internet, we display the author's name as "Why the Lucky Stiff" throughout this book, because the author refers to himself (on pages 15, 73, 108, and 165) as "Why". The title pages (1-3), however, are reproduced as accurately as possible from the original cover art gif, found at https://poignant.guide, which present the name in lower case.

Naming things is hard.

Thankfully, we have both his prolific work and his sense of magic, silliness, wonder and fun riven deep into our community.

My main thanks are to Why for originally writing this book (and its permissive licensing, which lets us reprint this) and obviously Matz for the Ruby language which inspired this tome. I think it holds up remarkably well. The book *and* the language.

Most of the hard work putting this together was done by Emma, supported by her team at Consonance. I mostly read proofs and asked questions in an attempt to appear intelligent.

Thank you also to the fine folks at Cookpad and FreeAgent. Without their financial support in the weird "cancelling in-person events" times, you wouldn't have this book in your hands.

But mostly thanks to you, for signing up to this untried, quasi-conference, for attending in the past, for attending in the future. And for being nice to each other.

Andy Croll

Read This Paragraph

At my local Barnes and Noble, there is a huge wall of Java books just waiting to tip over and crush me one day. And one day it will. At the rate things are going, one day that bookcase will be tall enough to crush us all. It might even loop the world several times, crushing previous editions of the same Java books over and over again.

And This Paragraph Too

This is just a small Ruby book. It won't crush you. It's light as a feather (because I haven't finished it yet—hehe). And there's a reason this book will stay light: because Ruby is simple to learn.

But Don't Read This One!

Why's (Poignant) Guide to Ruby is released under the Attribution-ShareAlike License. So, yes, please distribute it and print it and read it leisurely in your housecoat. In fact, there will be a contest at the end of the book for Best Housecoat. It's a coveted award and you should feel honored to even read about it! (Especially if you are reading about it in your soon-to-be-prize-winning housecoat.)

Now Back to Your Regularly Scheduled Paragraph

I'll try not to feel utterly rejected if this book doesn't capture your fancy. I might experience a few long days of emptiness, accompanied with profuse weeping, but other than that I'll be fine. It's at least comforting to know that the following fine texts cover my topic and will doubtless fill you with Ruby lust:

LEARNING TO PROGRAM
http://pine.fm/LearnToProgram/

A very basic, ground-level tutorial for the beginner to Ruby. By Chris Pine.

PROGRAMMING RUBY
http://pragprog.com/book/ruby3/programming-ruby-1-9

The original tome and complete reference for Ruby. By Dave Thomas and Andy Hunt (also known as The Pickaxe)

RUBY USER'S GUIDE
Ruby User's Guide

A guide to learning Ruby (with code examples). By Matz, the creator of Ruby. Translated into English.

RUBY-LANG.ORG
http://www.ruby-lang.org/

The official home page for the Ruby language.

Now, if you can't seem to find the contents link on the left-hand side of the page, then here's a link[1] to the first page of the (Poignant) Guide.

Welcome to the pirate radio of technical manuals.

---

1 Publisher's note: for this edition, substitute this sentence with 'please turn the page'.

About this Book

Kon'nichi wa, Ruby

1. Opening This Book

Pretend that you've opened this book (although you probably *have* opened this book), just to find a huge onion right in the middle crease of the book. (The manufacturer of the book has included the onion at my request.)

So you're like, "Wow, this book comes with an onion!" (Even if you don't particularly like onions, I'm sure you can appreciate the logistics of shipping any sort of produce discreetly inside of an alleged programming manual.)

Then you ask yourself, "Wait a minute. I thought this was a book on Ruby, the incredible new programming language from Japan. And although I can appreciate the logistics of shipping any sort of produce discreetly inside of an alleged programming manual: Why an onion? What am I supposed to do with it?"

No. Please don't puzzle over it. You don't need to do anything with the onion. Set the onion aside and let *it* do something with *you*.

I'll be straight with you. I want you to cry.

To weep. To whimper sweetly. This book is a **poignant** guide to Ruby. That means code so beautiful that tears are shed. That means gallant tales and somber truths that have you waking up the next morning in the arms of this book. Hugging it tightly to you all the day long. If necessary, fashion a makeshift hip holster for *Why's (Poignant) Guide to Ruby*, so you can always have this book's tender companionship.

You really must sob once. Or at least sniffle. And if not, then the onion will make it all happen for you.

2. The Dog Story

So try this first bit of poignancy on for size:

One day I was walking down one of those busy roads covered with car dealerships (this was shortly after my wedding was called off) and I found an orphaned dog on the road. A woolly, black dog with greenish red eyes. I was kind of feeling like an orphan myself, so I took a couple balloons that were tied to a pole at the dealership and I relocated them to the dog's collar. Then, I decided he would be my dog. I named him Bigelow.

We set off to get some Milkbones for Bigelow and, afterwards, head over to my place, where we could sit in recliners and listen to Gorky's Zygotic Mynci. Oh, and we'd also need to stop by a thrift store and get Bigelow his own recliner.

But Bigelow hadn't accepted me as his master. So five minutes later, the stupid dog took a different crosswalk than I did and I never caught up. So whereas he had previously only been lost once, he was now lost twice. I slowed my pace towards the life of Milkbones and an extra recliner. I had a dog for five minutes.

Stupid Benedict Arnold of a dog. I sat on a city bench and threw pine cones at a statue of three sheep crossing a bridge. After that, I wept for hours. The tears just came. Now there's a little something poignant to get you started.

I wonder where he went with all those balloons. That crazy dog must have looked like a party with legs.

It wasn't much later that I pulled my own Bigelow. I printed out a bunch of pages on Ruby. Articles found around the Web. I scanned through them on a train ride home one day. I flipped through them for five minutes and then gave up. Not impressed.

I sat, staring out the window at the world, a life-sized blender mixing graffiti and iron smelts before my eyes. *This world's too big for such a little language*, I thought. *Poor little thing doesn't stand a chance. Doesn't have legs to stand on. Doesn't have arms to swim.*

And yet, there I was. One little man on a flimsy little train (and I even still had a baby tooth to lose at the time) out of billions of people living on a floating blue rock. How can I knock Ruby? Who's to say that I'm not going to happen to choke on my cell phone and die later that evening. Why's dead, Ruby lives on.

The gravestone:

> *What's in his trachea?*
> *Oh, look, a Nokia!*

Just my luck. Finally get to have a good, long sleep underground, only to be constantly disturbed by *Pachelbel's Canon* going off in my stomach.

What I'm Going to Do With the Massive Proceeds from this Book

*A*nyone who's written a book can tell you how easily an author is distracted by visions of grandeur. In my experience, I stop twice for each paragraph, and four times for each panel of a comic, just to envision the wealth and prosperity that this book will procure for my lifestyle. I fear that the writing of this book will halt altogether to make way for the armada of SUVs and luxury town cars that are blazing away in my head.

Rather than stop my production of the (Poignant) Guide, I've reserved this space as a safety zone for pouring my empty and vain wishes.

Today I was at this Italian restaurant, Granado's, and I was paying my bill. Happened to notice (under glass) a bottle of balsamic vinegar going for $150. Fairly small. I could conceal it in my palm. Aged twenty-two years.

I've spent a lot of time thinking about that bottle. It is often an accessory in some of these obsessive fantasies. In one fantasy, I walk into the restaurant, toss a stack of greenery on the counter and earnestly say to the cashier, "Quick! I have an important salad to make!"

3. The Red Sun Rises

So, now you're wondering why I changed my mind about Ruby. The quick answer is: we clicked.

Like when you meet Somebody in college and they look like somebody who used to hit you in the face with paintbrushes when you were a kid. And so, impulsively, you conclude that this new Somebody is likely a non-friend. You wince at their hair. You hang up phones loudly during crucial moments in their anecdotes. You use your pogo stick right there where they are trying to walk!

Six months later, somehow, you and Somebody are sitting at a fountain having a perfectly good chat. Their face doesn't look so much like that childhood nemesis. You've met the Good Twin. You clicked.

So whereas I should probably be pounding your teeth in with hype about Ruby and the tightly-knit cadre of pertinent acronyms that accompany it everywhere (whetting the collective whistles of your bosses and their bosses' bosses), instead I will just let you coast. I'll let you free-fall through some code, interjecting occasionally with my own heartfelt experiences. It'll be quite easy, quite natural.

I should offer you some sort of motivation, though. So, Smotchkkiss, I'm going to give my three best reasons to learn Ruby and be done with it.

1. **Brain health.**
   Vitamin R. Goes straight to the head. Ruby will teach you to *express* your ideas through a computer. You will be writing stories for a machine.

   Creative skills, people. Deduction. Reason. Nodding intelligently. The language will become a tool for you to better connect your mind to the world. I've noticed that many experienced users of Ruby seem to be clear thinkers and objective. (In contrast to: heavily biased and coarse.)

2. **One man on one island.**
Ruby was born in Japan. Which is freaky. Japan is not known for its software. And since programming languages are largely written in English, who would suspect a language to come from Japan?

And yet, here we have Ruby. Against the odds, Yukihiro Matsumoto created Ruby on February 24, 1993. For the past ten years, he has steadily brought Ruby to a global audience. It's triumphant and noble and all that. Support diversity. Help us tilt the earth just a bit.

3. **Free.**
Using Ruby costs nothing. The code to Ruby itself is open for all of the world to inhale/exhale. Heck, this book is free. It's all part of a great, big giveaway that should have some big hitch to it.

You'd think we'd make you buy vacuums or timeshare or fake Monets. You'd think there'd be a 90 minute presentation where the owner of the company comes out at the end and knuckles you into sealing the deal.

Nope, free.

In another, related fantasy, I am throwing away lettuce. Such roughage isn't befitting of my new vinegar. No, I will have come to a point where the fame and the aristocracy will have corrupted me to my core. My new lettuce will be cash. Cold, hard cash, Mrs. Price.

Soon, I will be expending hundreds for a block of myzithra cheese.

My imaginations have now gone beyond possessions, though. Certainly, I have thought through my acquisition of Grecian urns, motorcades, airlines, pyramids, dinosaur bones. Occasionally I'll see wind-tossed cities on the news and I'll jot down on my shopping list: Hurricane.

But, now I'm seeing a larger goal. Simply put: what if I amassed such a fortune that the mints couldn't print enough to keep up with my demand? So, everyone else would be forced to use Monopoly money as actual currency. And you would have to win in Monopoly to keep food on the table. These would be some seriously tense games. I mean you go to mortgage St. James Place and your kids start crying. In addition, I think you'll begin to see the end of those who choose to use the Free Parking square as the underground coffers[1] for city funds.

1 http://groups.yahoo.com/group/monopoly/message/37

With that, it's time for the book to begin. You can now get out your highlighter and start dragging it along each captivating word from this sentence on. I think I have enough hairspray and funny money on my person to keep me sustained until the final page.

4. How Books Start

Now, if you ever have read a book, you know that no book can properly start without an exorbitant amount of synergy. Yes, synergy. Maybe you didn't know this. Synergy means that you and I are supposed to cooperate to make this a great reading experience.

We start off the book by getting along well in the Introduction. This togetherness, this **synergy**, propels us through the book, with me guiding you on your way. You give me a reassuring nod or snicker to indicate your progress.

I'm Peter Pan holding your hand. Come on, Wendy! Second star to the right and on till morning.

One problem here. I don't get along well with people. I don't hold hands very well.

Any of my staff will tell you. At the Opening Ceremonies of This Book (a catered event with stadium seating), I discovered that the cucumber sandwiches weren't served in tea towels. As a result, the butter hadn't set with the cucumbers right... Anyways, I made a big scene and set fire to some of the advertising trucks outside. I smashed this spotlight to pieces and so on. I had this loud maniacal laughing thing going on deep into that night. It was a real mess.

But, since I don't get along well with people, I hadn't invited anyone but myself to the Opening Ceremonies of This Book. So it wasn't really that embarrassing. I kept it under wraps and no one found out about the whole ordeal.

So you've got to know that **synergy** doesn't actually mean **synergy** in this book. I can't do normal **synergy**. No, in this book, **synergy** means **cartoon foxes**. What I'm saying is: this book will be starting off with an exorbitant amount of **cartoon foxes**.

And I will be counting on you to turn them into **synergy**.

You've got to hand it to fun money, though. Fake money rules. You can get your hands on it so quickly. For a moment, it seems like you're crazy rich. When I was a kid, I got with some of the neighborhood kids and we built this little Tijuana on our street. We made our own pesos and wore sombreros and everything!

*One kid was selling hot tamales for two pesos each. **Two pesos!** Did this kid know that the money was fake? Was he out of his mind? Who invited this kid? Didn't he know this wasn't really Tijuana? Maybe he was really from Tijuana! Maybe these were **real** pesos! Let's go make more **real** pesos!*

I think we even had a tavern where you could get totally hammered off Kool-Aid. There's nothing like a bunch of kids stumbling around, mumbling incoherently with punchy red clown lips.

A Quick (and Hopefully Painless) Ride Through Ruby (with Cartoon Foxes)

The foxes show up.

Yeah, these are the two. My asthma's kickin' in so I've got to go take a puff of medicated air just now. Be with you in a moment.

Foxes in boxes.

I'm told that this chapter is best accompanied by a rag. Something you can mop your face with as the sweat pours off your face.

Indeed, we'll be racing through the whole language. Like striking every match in a box as quickly as can be done.

1. Language and I MEAN Language

Our friends, those two helpless foxies, finally realize the gravity of their predicament.

My conscience won't let me call Ruby a *computer* language. That would imply that the language works primarily on the computer's terms. That the language is designed to accommodate the computer, first and foremost. That therefore, we, the coders, are foreigners, seeking citizenship in the computer's locale. It's the computer's language and we are translators for the world.

But what do you call the language when your brain begins to think in that language? When you start to use the language's own words and colloquialisms to express yourself. Say, the computer can't do that. How can it be the computer's language? It is ours, we speak it natively!

We can no longer truthfully call it a *computer* language. It is *coderspeak*. It is the language of our thoughts.

Read the following aloud to yourself.

```
5.times { print "Odelay!" }
```

In English sentences, punctuation (such as periods, exclamations, parentheses) are silent. Punctuation adds meaning to words, helps give cues as to what the author intended by a sentence. So let's read the above as: *Five times print "Odelay!".*

Which is exactly what this small Ruby program does. Beck's mutated Spanish exclamation will print five times on the computer screen.

Read the following aloud to yourself.

```
exit unless "restaurant".include? "aura"
```

Here we're doing a basic reality check. Our program will **exit** (the program will end) **unless** the word **restaurant** contains (or **includes**) the word **aura**. Again, in English: *Exit unless the word restaurant includes the word aura.*

Ever seen a programming language use question marks so effectively? Ruby uses some punctuation, such as exclamations and question marks, to enhance readability of the code. We're asking a question in the above code, so why not make that apparent?

Read the following aloud to yourself.

```
['toast', 'cheese', 'wine'].each {|food| print food.capitalize }
```

While this bit of code is less readable and sentence-like than the previous examples, I'd still encourage you to read it aloud. While Ruby may sometimes read like English, it sometimes reads as a shorter English. Fully translated into English, you might read the above as: *With the words 'toast', 'cheese', and 'wine': take each food and print it capitalized.*

The computer then courteously responds: **Toast, Cheese** and **Wine**.

At this point, you're probably wondering how these words actually fit together. Smotchkkiss is wondering what the dots and brackets mean. I'm going to discuss the various *parts of speech* next.

All you need to know thus far is that Ruby is basically built from sentences. They aren't exactly English sentences. They are short collections of words and punctuation which encompass a single thought. These sentences can form books. They can form pages. They can form entire novels, when strung together. Novels that can be read by humans, but also by computers.

Concerning Commercial Uses of the (Poignant) Guide

This book is released under a Creative Commons license which allows unlimited commercial use of this text. Basically, this means you can sell all these bootleg copies of my book and keep the revenues for yourself. I trust my readers (and the world around them) to rip me off. To put out some crappy Xerox edition with that time-tested clipart of praying hands on the cover.

Guys, the lawsuits just ain't worth the headache. So I'm just going to straight up endorse authorized piracy, folks. Anybody who wants to read the book should be able to read it. Anybody who wants to market the book or come up with special editions, I'm flattered.

Why would I want the $$$? IGNORE ALL OTHER SIDEBARS: I've lost the will to be a rich slob. Sounds inhuman, but I like my little black-and-white television. Also my hanging plastic flower lamp. I don't want to be a career writer. Cash isn't going inspire me. Pointless.

So, if money means nothing to the lucky stiff, why rip me off when you could co-opt shady business practices to literally crush my psyche and leave me wheezing in some sooty iron lung? Oh, and the irony of using my own works against me! Die, Poignant Boy!

To give you an idea of what I mean, here are a few underhanded concepts that could seriously kill my willpower and force me to reconsider things like existence.

IDEA ONE: BIG TOBACCO

Buy a cigarette company. Use my cartoon foxes to fuel an aggressive ad campaign. Here's a billboard for starters:

Addiction is like Pokémon!

Make it obvious that you're targeting children and the asthmatic. Then, once you've got everyone going, have the **truth** people do an expose on me and my farm of inky foxes.

Sensible Hipster Standing on Curb in Urban Wilderness: He calls himself the lucky stiff.

(Pulls aside curtain to reveal gray corpse on a gurney.)

Hipster: Some stiffs ain't so lucky.

(Erratic zoom in. Superimposed cartoon foxes for subliminal Willy Wonka mind trip.)

Yo. Why you gotta dis Big Smokies like dat, Holmes?

IDEA TWO: HEY, FIRING SQUAD

Like I said, start selling copies of my book, but corrupt the text. These altered copies would contain numerous blatant (and libelous) references to government agencies, such as the U.S. Marshals and the Pentagon. You could make me look like a complete traitor. Like I have all these plans to, you know, kill certain less desirable members of the U.S. Marshals or the Pentagon.

Not that there are any less desirable members of the U.S. Marshals or the Pentagon. Yeah, I didn't mean it like that.

Oh, crap.

Oh, crap. Oh, crap. Oh, crap.

Turn off the lights. Get down.

IDEA THREE: BILLBOARDS, PART II

How about making fun of asthmatics directly?

Call it a puffer! ROFL!

IDEA FOUR: ALEC BALDWIN

Adapt the book into a movie. And since, you know, I'm a character in this book, you could get someone like Alec Baldwin to play me. Someone who's at a real low point in his career.

You could make it seem like I did tons of drugs. Like I was insane to work with. Like I kept firing people and locking them in the scooter room and making them wear outfits made of bread. Yeah, like I could actually be **baking** people into the outfits.

You could have this huge mold that I strap people into. Then, I pour all the dough on them and actually bake them until the bread has risen and they've almost died. And when the television crews come and I'm on Good Morning America, they'll ask, "So, how many people have you employed in the production of your book?" And I'd respond, "A baker's dozen!" and erupt into that loud maniacal laughing that would force audience members to cup their hands over their ears.

Of course, in the throes of my insanity, I would declare war on the world. The bread people would put up quite a fight. Until the U.S. Marshals (or the Pentagon) engineer a giant robotic monkey brain (played by Burt Lancaster) to come after me.

Here's where you'll make me look completely lame. Not only will I sacrifice all of the bread people (the Starchtroopers) to save myself, not only will I surrender to the great monkey brain like a coward, but when I narrowly escape, I'll yell at the audience. Screaming insistently that it's **MY** movie and no one should see it any more, I'll rip the screen in half and the film projector will spin with its reel flapping in defeat. And that will be the end of the movie. People will be **so** pissed.

Now, I've got to thinking. See, and actually, Alec Baldwin did a decent voiceover in **The Royal Tenenbaums**. His career might be okay. You might not want to use him. He might not do it.

Tell ya what. I'll play the part. I've made a career out of low points.

2. The Parts of Speech

Just like the white stripe down a skunk's back and the winding, white train of a bride, many of Ruby's parts of speech have visual cues to help you identify them. Punctuation and capitalization will help your brain to see bits of code and feel intense recognition. Your mind will frequently yell *Hey, I know that guy!* You'll also be able to name-drop in conversations with other Rubyists.

Try to focus on the look of each of these parts of speech. The rest of the book will detail the specifics. I give short descriptions for each part of speech, but you don't have to understand the explanation. By the end of this chapter, you should be able to recognize every part of a Ruby program.

Variables

Any plain, lowercase word is a variable in ruby. Variables may consist of letters, digits and underscores.

x, y, banana2 or **phone_a_quail** are examples.

Variables are like nicknames. Remember when everyone used to call you Stinky Pete? People would say, "Get over here, Stinky Pete!" And everyone miraculously knew that Stinky Pete was you.

With variables, you give a nickname to something you use frequently. For instance, let's say you run an orphanage. It's a mean orphanage. And whenever Daddy Warbucks comes to buy more kids, we insist that he pay us **one-hundred twenty-one dollars and eight cents** for the kid's teddy bear, which the kid has become attached to over in the darker moments of living in such nightmarish custody.

```
teddy_bear_fee = 121.08
```

Later, when you ring him up at the cash register (a really souped-up cash register which runs Ruby!), you'll need to add together all his charges into a **total**.

```
total = orphan_fee + teddy_bear_fee + gratuity
```

Those variable nicknames sure help. And in the seedy underground of child sales, any help is appreciated I'm sure.

They mock my examples.

Numbers

The most basic type of number is an *integer*, a **series of digits** which can start with a **plus or minus sign**.

1, **23**, and **-10000** are examples.

Commas are not allowed in numbers, but underscores are. So if you feel the need to mark your thousands so the numbers are more readable, use an underscore.

```
population = 12_000_000_000
```

Decimal numbers are called *floats* in Ruby. Floats consist of numbers with **a decimal place** or **scientific notation**.

3.14, **-808.08** and **12.043e-04** are examples.

Strings

Strings are any sort of characters (letters, digits, punctuation) surrounded by quotes. Both single and double **quotes** are used to create strings.

"sealab", **'2021'**, or **"These cartoons are hilarious!"** are examples.

When you enclose characters in quotes, they are stored together as a single string.

Think of a reporter who is jotting down the mouth noises of a rambling celebrity. "I'm a lot wiser," says Avril Lavigne. "Now I know what the business is like—what you have to do and how to work it."

```
avril_quote = "I'm a lot wiser.  Now I know
what the business is like -- what you have
to do and how to work it."
```

So, just as we stored a number in the **teddy_bear_fee** variable, now we're storing a collection of characters (a string) in the **avril_quote** variable. The reporter sends this quote to the printers, who just happen to use Ruby to operate their printing press.

```ruby
print oprah_quote
print avril_quote
print ashlee_simpson_debacle
```

Symbols

Symbols are words that look just like variables. Again, they may contain letters, digits, or underscores. But they **start with a colon**.

:a, :b, or :ponce_de_leon are examples.

Symbols are lightweight strings. Usually, symbols are used in situations where you

They desire to be in my examples.

need a string but you won't be printing it to the screen.

You could say a symbol is a bit easier on the computer. It's like an antacid. The colon indicates the bubbles trickling up from your computer's stomach as it digests the symbol. Ah. Sweet, sweet relief.

Constants

Constants are words like variables, but constants are **capitalized**. If variables are the nouns of Ruby, then think of constants as the proper nouns.

Time, **Array** or **Bunny_Lake_is_Missing** are examples.

In English, proper nouns are capitalized. The Empire State Building. You can't just move The Empire State Building. You can't just decide that the Empire State Building is something else. Proper nouns are

Chunky bacon!!

like that. They refer to something very specific and usually don't change over time.

In the same way, constants can't be changed after they are set.

```
EmpireStateBuilding = "350 5th Avenue, NYC, NY"
```

If we try to change the constant, Ruby will complain to us. Such things are frowned upon.

Methods

If variables and constants are the nouns, then methods are the verbs. Methods are usually attached to the end of variables and constants by a **dot**. You've already seen methods at work.

Come on, chunky bacon.

```
front_door.open
```

In the above, **open** is the method. It is the action, the verb. In some cases, you'll see actions chained together.

```
front_door.open.close
```

We've instructed the computer to open the front door and then immediately close it.

```
front_door.is_open?
```

The above is an action as well. We're instructing the computer to test the door to see if it's open. The method could be called **Door.test_to_see_if_its_open**, but the **is_open?** name is succinct and just as correct. Both exclamation marks and question marks may be used in method names.

Method arguments

A method may require more information in order to perform its action. If we want the computer to paint the door, we should provide a color as well.

Method arguments are attached to the end of a method. The arguments are usually surrounded by **parentheses** and separated by **commas**.

```
front_door.paint( 3, :red )
```

The above paints the front door 3 coats of red.

Think of it as an inner tube the method is pulling along, containing its extra instructions. The parentheses form the wet, round edges of the inner tube. The commas are the feet of each argument, sticking over the edge. The last argument has its feet tucked under so they don't show.

Like a boat pulling many inner tubes, methods with arguments can be chained.

```
front_door.paint( 3, :red ).dry( 30 ).close()
```

The above paints the front door 3 coats of red, dries for 30 minutes, and closes the door. Even though the last method has no arguments, you can still put parentheses if you like. There is no use dragging an empty inner tube, so the parentheses are normally dropped.

Some methods (such as **print**) are kernel methods. These methods are used throughout Ruby. Since they are so common, you won't use the dot.

```
print "See, no dot."
```

Class methods

Like the methods described above (also called *instance* methods), class methods are usually attached after variables and constants. Rather than a dot, a **double colon** is used.

```
Door::new( :oak )
```

As seen above, the **new** class method is most often used to create things. In the above example, we're asking Ruby to make a new oak door for us. Of course, Ruby has to have an understanding of how to make a door—as well as a wealth of timber, lumberjacks, and those long, wiggly, two-man saws.

Global variables

Variables which begin with a **dollar sign** are global.

$x, **$1**, **$chunky** and **$CHunKY_ bACOn** are examples.

Plenty of chunky bacon to go around.

Most variables are rather temporary in nature. Some parts of your program are like little houses. You walk in and they have their own variables. In one house, you may have a **dad** that represents Archie, a traveling salesman and skeleton collector. In another house, **dad** could represent Peter, a lion tamer with a great love for flannel. Each house has its own meaning for **dad**.

With global variables, you can be guaranteed that the variable is the same in every little house. The dollar sign is very appropriate. Every American home respects the value of the dollar. We're crazy for the stuff. Try knocking on any door in America and hand them cash. I can guarantee you won't get the same reaction if you knock on a door and offer Peter, a lion tamer with a great love for flannel.

Global variables can be used anywhere in your program. They never go out of sight.

Instance variables

Variables which begin with an **at** symbol are instance variables.

`@x`, `@y`, and `@only_the_chunkiest_cut_of_bacon_I_ have_ever_seen` are examples.

These variables are often used to define the attributes of something. For example, you might provide Ruby with the width of the `front_door` by setting the `@width` variable inside that `front_door`. Instance variables are used to define characteristics of a single object in Ruby.

Think of the **at** symbol as meaning **attribute**.

Class variables

Variables which begin with **double at** symbols are class variables.

`@@x`, `@@y`, and `@@i_will_take_your_chunky_bacon_and_ raise_you_two` are examples.

Class variables, too, are used to define attributes. But rather than defining an attribute for a single object in Ruby, class variables give an attribute to many related objects in Ruby. If instance variables set attributes for a single `front_door`, then class variables set attributes for everything that is a `Door`.

Think of the **double at** prefix as meaning **attribute all**. Additionally, you can think of a swarm of **AT-ATs** from *Star Wars*, which are all commanded by Ruby. You change a class variable and not just one changes, they all change.

Woohoo! Chunky bacon accomplished!

Blocks

Any code surrounded by **curly braces** is a block.

```
2.times {
  print "Yes, I've used chunky bacon in my examples, but
never again!"
}
```

With blocks, you can group a set of instructions together so that they can be passed around your program. The curly braces give the appearance of crab pincers that have snatched the code and are holding it together. When you see these two pincers, remember that the code inside has been pressed into a single unit.

It's like one of those little Hello Kitty boxes they sell at the mall that's stuffed with tiny pencils and microscopic paper, all crammed into a glittery transparent case that can be concealed in your palm for covert stationery operations. Except that blocks don't require so much squinting.

The curly braces can also be traded for the words **do** and **end**, which is nice if your block is longer than one line.

```
loop do
  print "Much better."
  print "Ah.  More space!"
  print "My back was killin' me in those crab pincers."
end
```

Block arguments

Block arguments are a set of variables surrounded by **pipe** characters and separated by **commas**.

|x|, **|x,y|**, and **|up, down, all_around|** are examples.

Block arguments are used at the beginning of a block.

```
{ |x,y| x + y }
```

In the above example, **|x,y|** are the arguments. After the arguments, we have a bit of code. The expression **x + y** adds the two arguments together.

I like to think of the pipe characters as representing a tunnel. They give the appearance of a chute that the variables are sliding down. (An **x** goes down spread eagle, while the **y** neatly crosses her legs.) This chute acts as a passageway between blocks and the world around them.

Variables are passed through this chute (or tunnel) into the block.

And then, the dismal truth.

Ranges

A range is two values surrounded by **parentheses** and separated by **an ellipsis** (in the form of two or three dots).

- **(1..3)** is a range, representing the numbers 1 through 3.

- **('a'..'z')** is a range, representing a lowercase alphabet.

Think of it as an accordion which has been squeezed down for carrying. (Sure, you can build a great sense of self-worth by carrying around an unfolded accordion, but sometimes a person needs to wallow in self-doubt, carefully concealing the squeeze-box.) The parentheses are the handles on the sides of a smaller, handheld accordion. The dots are the chain, keeping the folds tightly closed.

Normally, only two dots are used. If a third dot is used, the last value in the range is excluded.

- **(0...5)** represents the numbers 0 through 4.

When you see that third dot, imagine opening the accordion slightly. Just enough to let one note from its chamber. The note is that end value. We'll let the sky eat it.

Arrays

An array is a list surrounded by **square brackets** and separated by **commas**.

- `[1, 2, 3]` is an array of numbers.

- `['coat', 'mittens', 'snowboard']` is an array of strings.

Think of it as a caterpillar which has been stapled into your code. The two square brackets are staples which keep the caterpillar from moving, so you can keep track of which end is the head and which is the tail. The commas are the caterpillar's legs, wiggling between each section of its body.

Once there was a caterpillar who had commas for legs. Which meant he had to allow a literary pause after each step. The other caterpillars really respected him for it and he came to have quite a commanding presence. Oh, and talk about a philanthropist! He was notorious for giving fresh leaves to those less-fortunate.

Yes, an array is a collection of things, but it also keeps those things in a specific order.

Hashes

A hash is a dictionary surrounded by **curly braces**. Dictionaries match words with their definitions. Ruby does so with **arrows** made from an equals sign, followed by a greater-than sign.

`{'a' => 'aardvark', 'b' => 'badger'}` is an example.

This time, the curly braces represent little book symbols. See how they look like little, open books with creases down the middle? They represent opening and closing our dictionary.

Imagine our dictionary has a definition on each of its pages. The commas represent the corner of each page, which we turn to see the next definition. And on each page: a word followed by an arrow pointing to the definition.

```
{ 'name' => 'Peter', 'profession' => 'lion tamer',
  'great love' => 'flannel' }
```

I'm not comparing hashes to dictionaries because you can only store definitions in a hash. In the example above, I stored personal information for Peter, the lion tamer with a great love for flannel. Hashes are like dictionaries because they can be very easy to search through.

The foxes think silence will kill the comic.

Regular Expressions

A regular expression (or *regexp*) is a set of characters surrounded by **slashes**.

/ruby/, **/[0-9]+/** and **/^\d{3}-\d{3}-\d{4}/** are examples.

Regular expressions are used to find words or patterns in text. The slashes on each side of the expression are pins.

Imagine if you had a little word with pins on both side and you held it over a book. You pass the word over the book and when it gets near a matching word, it starts blinking. You pin the regular expression onto the book, right over the match and it glows with the letters of the matching word.

Oh, and when you poke the pins into the book, the paper sneezes, *reg-exp!*

Regular expressions are much faster than passing your hand over pages of a book. Ruby can use a regular expression to search volumes of books very quickly.

Operators

You'll use the following list of operators to do math in Ruby or to compare things. Scan over the list, recognize a few. You know, addition **+** and subtraction **-** and so on.

```
**  !   ~   *   /   %   +   -   &
<<  >>  |   ^   >   >=  <   <=  <=>
||  !=  =~  !~  &&  +=  -=  ==  ===
..  ...  not and or
```

Keywords

Ruby has a number of built-in words, imbued with meaning. These words cannot be used as variables or changed to suit your purposes. Some of these we've already discussed. They are in the safe house, my friend. You touch these and you'll be served an official syntax error.

```
alias     and       BEGIN   begin   break    case     class
def       defined   do      else    elsif    END      end
ensure    false     for     if      in       module   next
nil       not       or      redo    rescue   retry    return
self      super     then    true    undef    unless   until
when      while     yield
```

Good enough. These are the illustrious members of the Ruby language. We'll be having quite the junket for the next three chapters, gluing these parts together into sly bits of (poignant) code.

I'd recommend skimming all of the parts of speech once again. Give yourself a broad view of them. I'll be testing your metal in the next section.

Out in the pickup truck.

Seven Moments of Zen from My Life

8 years old. Just laying in bed, thinking. And I realize. **There's nothing stopping me from becoming a child dentist.**

21. Found a pencil on the beach. Embossed on it: I **cherish serenity.** *Tucked it away into the inside breast pocket of my suit jacket. Watched the waves come and recede.*

22. Found a beetle in my bathroom that was just about to fall into a heating vent. Swiped him up. Tailored him a little backpack out of a leaf and a thread. In the backpack: a skittle and a AAA battery. That should last him. Set him loose out by the front gate.

Three years of age. Brushed aside the curtain. Sunlight.

14. Riding my bike out on the pier with my coach who is jogging behind me as the sun goes down right after I knocked out Piston Honda in the original Nintendo version of Mike Tyson's Punch-Out.

3. If I Haven't Treated You Like a Child Enough Already

I'm proud of you. Anyone will tell you how much I brag about you. How I go on and on about this great anonymous person out there who scrolls and reads and scrolls and reads[2]. "These kids," I tell them. "Man, these kids got heart. I never..." And I can't even finish a sentence because I'm absolutely blubbering.

And my heart glows bright red under my filmy, translucent skin and they have to administer 10cc of JavaScript to get me to come back. (I respond well to toxins in the blood.) Man, that stuff will kick the peaches right out your gills!

So, yes. You've kept up nicely. But now I must begin to be a brutal schoolmaster. I need to start seeing good marks from you. So far, you've done nothing but move your eyes around a lot. Okay, sure, you did some exceptional reading aloud earlier. Now we need some comprehension skills here, Smotchkkiss.

Say aloud each of the parts of speech used below.

```
5.times { print "Odelay!" }
```

You might want to even cover this paragraph up while you read, because your eyes might want to sneak to the answer. We have a *number* **5**, followed by a *method* **.times**. Then, the first crab pincers of a *block*. The kernel *method* **print** has no dot and is followed by a *string* **"Odelay!"**. The final crab pincers close our *block*.

---

2 Publisher's note: for this edition, substitute this sentence with "turns pages".

Say aloud each of the parts of speech used below.

```
exit unless "restaurant".include?
"aura"
```

Like the **print** method, **exit** is a kernel *method*. If you were paying attention during the big list of keywords, you'll know that **unless** is just such a *keyword*. The *string* **"restaurant"** is clung to by the *method* **include?**. And finally, the string **"aura"**.

Say aloud each of the parts of speech used below.

```
['toast', 'cheese', 'wine'].each { |food| print( food.capitalize ) }
```

This caterpillar partakes of finer delicacies. An *array* starts this example. In the array, three *strings* **'toast'**, **'cheese'**, and **'wine'**. The whole array is trailed by a *method* **each**.

Inside of a *block*, the *block argument* **food**, traveling down its little waterslide into the block. The *method* **capitalize** then capitalizes the first letter of the block argument, which has become *variable* **food**. This capitalized *string* is passed to kernel *method* **print**.

Look over these examples once again. Be sure you recognize the parts of speech used. They each have a distinct look, don't they? Take a deep breath, press firmly on your temples. Now, let's dissect a cow's eye worth of code.

11. Sick. Watching Heathcliff on television. For hours, it was Heathcliff. And he was able to come right up close to my face. His head spun toward me. His face pulsed back and forth, up close, then off millions of miles away. Sound was gone. In fractions of a second, Heathcliff filled the universe, then blipped off to the end of infinity. I heard my mother's voice trying to cut through the cartoon. Heathclose, Heathaway, Heathclose, Heathaway. It was a religious rave with a cat strobe and muffled bass of mother's voice. (I ran a fever of 105 that day.)

18. Bought myself a gigapet. A duck. Fed it for awhile. Gave it a bath. Forgot about it for almost a couple months. One day, while cleaning, I found a chain and he was there on the end. Hey, little duck. Mad freaky, hoppin' around with his hair out, squawking diagonal lines. In a tuxedo.

4. An Example to Help You Grow Up

Gettin' cabin fever.

Say aloud each of the parts of speech used below.

```
require 'net/http'
Net::HTTP.start( 'www.ruby-lang.org', 80 ) do |http|
  print( http.get( '/en/about/license.txt' ).body )
end
```

The first line is a method call. The *method* called **require** is used. A *string* is passed to the method containing **'net/http'**. Think of this first line of code as a sentence. We have told Ruby to load some helper code, the **Net::HTTP** library.

The next three lines all go together. The *constant* **Net::HTTP** refers to the library we loaded above. We are using the *method* **start** from the library. Into the method, we're sending a *string* **'www.ruby-lang.org'** and the *number* **80**.

The word **do** opens a *block*. The block has one *block variable* **http**. Inside the block, the *method* **print** is called. What is being printed?

From the *variable* **http**, the *method* **get** is called. Into **get**, we pass a *string* containing the path **'/en/about/license.txt'**. Now, notice that another method is chained onto **get**. The *method* **body**. Then, the block closes with **end**.

Doing okay? Just out of curiosity, can you guess what this example does? Hopefully, you're seeing some patterns in Ruby. If not, just shake your head vigorously while you've got these examples in your mind. The code should break apart into manageable pieces.

For example, this pattern is used a number of times:

```
_variable_ . _method_ ( _method arguments_ )
```

You see it inside the block:

```
http.get( '/en/about/license.txt' )
```

We're using Ruby to get a web page. You've probably used HTTP with your web browser. HTTP is the Hypertext Transfer Protocol. HTTP is used to transfer web pages across the Internet. Conceptualize a bus driver that can drive across the Internet and bring back web pages for us. On his hat are stitched the letters HTTP.

The variable **http** is that bus driver. The *method* is a message to the bus driver. Go **get** the web page called **/en/about/license.txt**.

So where you see the chain of methods:

```
http.get( '/en/about/license.txt' ).body
```

Since we'll be getting back a web page from the **http** bus driver, you can read this in your brain as:

```
_web page_ .body
```

And this bit of code:

```
print( http.get( '/en/about/license.txt' ).body )
```

This code gets the web page. We send a **body** message to the web page, which gives us all the HTML in a *string*. We then **print** that string. See how the basic dot-method pattern happens in a chain. The next chapter will explore all these sorts of patterns in Ruby. It'll be good fun.

So, what does this code do? It prints the Ruby license page to the screen using a web-enabled bus driver.

5. And So, The Quick Trip Came To An Eased, Cushioned Halt

Running after the truck.

So now we have a problem. I get the feeling that you are enjoying this way too much. And you haven't even hit the chapter where I use jump-roping songs to help you learn how to parse XML!

If you're already enjoying this, then things are really going bad. Two chapters from now you'll be writing your own Ruby programs. In fact, it's right about there that I'll have you start writing your own role-playing game, your own file-sharing network (a la BitTorrent), as well as a program that will pull genuine random numbers from the Internet.

And you know (you've got to know!) that this is going to turn into an obsession. First, you'll completely forget to take the dog out. It'll be standing by the screen door, darting its head about, as your eyes devour the code, as your fingers slip messages to the computer.

Thanks to your neglect, things will start to break. Your mounds of printed sheets of code will cover up your air vents. Your furnace will choke. The trash will pile-up: take-out boxes you hurriedly ordered in, junk mail you couldn't care to dispose of. Your own uncleanliness will pollute the air. Moss will infest the rafters, the water will clog, animals will let themselves in, trees will come up through the foundations.

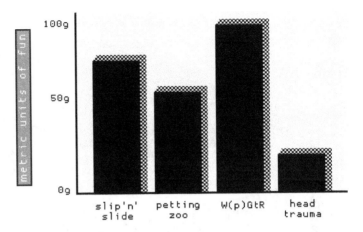

But your computer will be well-cared for. And you, Smotchkkiss, will have nourished it with your knowledge. In the eons you will have spent with your machine, you will have become part-CPU. And it will have become part-flesh. Your arms will flow directly into its ports. Your eyes will accept the video directly from DVI-24 pin. Your lungs will sit just above the processor, cooling it.

And just as the room is ready to force itself shut upon you, just as all the overgrowth swallows you and your machine, you will finish your script. You and the machine together will run this latest Ruby script, the product of your obsession. And the script will fire up chainsaws to trim the trees, hearths to warm and regulate the house. Builder nanites will rush from your script, reconstructing your quarters, retiling, renovating, chroming, polishing, disinfecting. Mighty androids will force your crumbling house into firm, rigid architecture. Great pillars will rise, statues chiseled. You will have dominion over this palatial estate and over the encompassing mountains and islands of your stronghold.

So I guess you're going to be okay. Whatdya say? Let's get moving on this script of yours?

Floating Little Leaves of Code

I've never seen the ham do anything but leak juice. Today, our business in Ambrose Caverns is with the elf. He is a crucial part of the next lessons. Let's all make him feel welcome. Go start warming up your listening hats! (And please change out of those ridiculous stirrup pants.)

A prompt warning: this lesson is much slower. Stay with it. This will be a long, deep breath. The most crucial stage of your instruction. It may seem like you're not learning much code at first. You will be learning concepts. By the end of this chapter, you will know Ruby's beauty. The coziness of the code will become a down sleeping bag for your own solace.

1. The Leaf as a Status Symbol in Ambrose

Alright, Elf. Give us a quick rundown of the currency issues you've faced there in your kingdom.

Blue Crystals got the shaft.

Yeah, that's not the way I remember it. This Elf was paging me constantly. When I refused to call him back, he somehow left a message on my pager. Meaning: it beeped a couple times and then printed out a small slip of paper. The slip said something to the effect of, "Get down here quick!" and also, "We've got to rid the earth of this scourge of entrepreneurial caterpillars, these twisted insect vikings are suffocating my blue crystals!"

Lately, the exchange rate has settled down between leaves and crystals. One tree-grown note is worth five crystals. So the basic money situation looks like this:

```
blue_crystal = 1
leaf_tender = 5
```

This example is, like, *totally* last chapter. Still. It's a start. We're setting two *variables*. The **equals sign** is used for *assignment*.

Now **leaf_tender** represents the number **5** (as in: five blue crystals.) This concept right here is **half of Ruby**. We're *defining*. We're *creating*. This is half of the work. Assignment is the most basic form of defining.

You can't complain though, can you Elf? You've built an empire from cashing your blue crystals into the new free market among the forest creatures. (And even though he's an elf to us, he's a tall monster to them.)

Animal Perfect, LLC

Nonono. Hang on a sec. You're not ready for what the Elf here is doing in his caves. You'll think it's all positively inhumane, naughty, sick, tweeested, yada yada.

The Scarf Eaters

I hate to intrude upon your instruction, but I've already walked all over it enough to warrant some further disregard. Can I go over my next project with you?

I've pledged to write another book. (Trombones.) The good news is that I won't actually be writing any of it. You won't have to endure any more of this inane blathering.

It's over between me and words. I'd love to stick around and exploit them each, one after another, but it's all becoming quite predictable, wouldn't you say? Eventually, they will all be used and I'd have to come up with fake words and that would be way too cnoofy.

Now. The deal isn't cut yet, but I'm in negotiations with Anna Quindlen to do my ghost writing. We're tag-teaming on a book that's going to blow the (Poignant) Guide right out of your hands. To put it bluntly, the Guide will be worthless. You won't be able to pile enough pomegranates on top of the thing.

So this new book. The Scarf Eaters. It's a coming-of-age novel. But it's also a beginner's guide to Macromedia Flash. It's like Judy Blume crossed Praystation. It's like Osil8 starring Hillary Duff.

I don't want to give away the plot at all, but to tug your appetite I'll just say this: one kid talks to his dead brother in ActionScript. More to come.

Now You're Going to Hear the Animal Perfect Mission Statement Because This Is A Book And We Have Time And No Rush, Right?

Back, back, way back before speedboats, I owned a prize race horse who took a stumble on the track. She did ten front flips and crashed into a guy who was carrying a full jar of mayonnaise. We had blood and mayonnaise up and down the track. Needless to say, she was a disaster.

The vet took one look at her and swore she'd never walk again. Her legs were gone and the vet wouldn't allow a legless horse to just sit around. We'd need to put her down. He swore his life and career on it, insisting we divide into two parallel lines. The people who could not refute the doctor's claims on one side; those too stubborn to accept his infallible medical reasoning on the other. The Elf, his pet ham, and I were the only ones in that second line.

So while the others heaped up trophies and great wreaths around the horse, bidding it a fond farewell before the bullet came to take him home, the Elf and I frantically pawed the Internet for answers. We took matter into our own hands, cauterizing her leg wounds with live crawdads. It worked great! We now had a horse again. Or at least: a horse body with a crustaceous abdominal frosting.

She scurried everywhere after that and lived for years in pleasantly moist underground cavities.

Animal Perfect is now the future of animal enhancement. They build new animals and salvage old-style animals for parts. Of course, they've come a long ways. When Animal Perfect started, you'd see a full-grown bear walk into Animal Perfect and you'd see a full-grown bear with sunglasses walk out. Completely cheesy.

Stick around and you'll see a crab with *his own jet pack*. That's a new 2004 model jetcrab.

But now, the whole operation is up and running. And the cleanliness of the place is astonishing. All the equipment is so shiny. Everything is in chrome. Oh, and all the staff have concealed weapons. They're trained to kill anyone who enters unannounced. Or, if they run out of bullets, they're trained to pistol whip anyone who enters unannounced.

Elf, make me a starmonkey.

First, the star is caught.

Some imaginary Ruby for you:

```
pipe.catch_a_star
```

Variable **pipe**. Method **catch_a_star**. A lot of Rubyists like to think of methods as a message. Whatever comes before the dot is handed the message. The above code tells the **pipe** to **catch_a_star**.

This is the **second half** of Ruby. Putting things in motion. These things you define and create in the first half start to *act* in the second half.

1. Defining things.
2. Putting those things into action.

So what if the star catching code works? Where does the star go?

```
captive_star = pipe.catch_a_star
```

See, it's up to you to collect the miserable, little star. If you don't, it'll simply vanish. Whenever you use a method, you'll always be given something back. You can ignore it or use it.

*If you can learn to use the answers that methods give you back, then you will **dominate**.*

Star is ratcheted to the monkey's face.

Quickly then.

```
starmonkey = ratchet.attach( captive_monkey, captive_star )
```

The **ratchet** gets an **attach** message. What needs to be attached? The *method arguments*: the **captive_monkey** and the **captive_star**. We are given back a **starmonkey**, which we have decided to hang on to.

Frog on the hand.

This is turning out to be such a short, little proggie that I'm just going to put it all together as one statement.

```
starmonkey = ratchet.attach( captive_monkey, pipe.catch_a_star )
+ deco_hand_frog
```

See how **pipe.catch_a_star** is right in the arguments for the method? The caught star will get passed right to the ratchet. No need to find a place to put it. Just let it go.

2. Small and Nearly Worthless

DOWN IN THE AMBROSE CAVERNS BREAK ROOM...

Law-va.

The hotel here in Ambrose is no good at all. The beds are all lumpy. The elevator is tiny. One guy put all his bags in the elevator and found out there wasn't room for him. He hit the button and chased up the stairs after it all. But the stairwell turned out to be too narrow and his shoulders got wedged going up.

The soap mini-bars they give you are sized down for elves, so it's impossible to work up a lather. I hate it. I keep mistaking them for contact lenses.

I turned on the faucet and nothing came out. Thing is: Ambrose is a place with magical properties, so I took a chance. I put my hands under the spigot. Invisible, warm wetness. I felt the hurried sensation of running water, darting through my fingers. When I took my hands away, they were dry and clean.

It was an amazing nothingness to experience. It was just like **nil**.

Nil

In Ruby, **nil** represents an emptiness. It is **without value**. It isn't zero. Zero is a number.

It's Ruby's own walking dead, a flatlined keyword. You can't add to it, it doesn't evolve. But it's terribly popular. This skeleton's smiling in all the pictures.

```
plastic_cup = nil
```

The above **plastic_cup** is **empty**. You could argue that the **plastic_cup** contains something, a **nil**. The **nil** represents the emptiness, though, so go ahead and call it empty.

Some of you who have programmed before will be tempted to say the **plastic_cup** is **undefined**. How about let's not. When you say a variable is undefined, you're saying that Ruby simply has no recollection of the variable, it doesn't know the var, it's absolutely non-existent.

But Ruby is aware of the **plastic_cup**. Ruby can easily look in the **plastic_cup**. It's **empty**, but not **undefined**.

False

The cat Trady Blix. Frozen in emptiness. Immaculate whiskers rigid. Placid eyes of lake. Tail of warm icicle. Sponsored by a Very Powerful Pause Button.

The darkness surrounding Blix can be called **negative space**. Hang on to that phrase. Let it suggest that the emptiness has a negative connotation. In a similar way, **nil** has a slightly sour note that it whistles.

Generally speaking, **everything in Ruby has a positive charge to it**. This spark flows through strings, numbers, regexps, all of it. Only two keywords wear a shady cloak: **nil** and **false** draggin' us down.

You can **test that charge** with an **if** keyword. It looks very much like the **do** blocks we saw in the last chapter, in that both end with an **end**.

```
if plastic_cup
  print "Plastic cup is on the up 'n' up!"
end
```

If **plastic_cup** contains either **nil** or **false**, you won't see anything print to the screen. They're not on the **if** guest list. So **if** isn't going to run any of the code it's protecting.

But **nil** and **false** need not walk away in shame. They may be of questionable character, but **unless** runs a smaller establishment that caters to the bedraggled. The **unless** keyword has a policy of **only allowing those with a negative charge in**. Who are: **nil** and **false**.

```
unless plastic_cup
  print "Plastic cup is on the down low."
end
```

You can also use **if** and **unless** at the **end of a single line of code**, if that's all that is being protected.

```
print "Yeah, plastic cup is up again!" if plastic_cup
print "Hardly. It's down." unless plastic_cup
```

And another nice trick: stack the **if** and **unless**.

```
print "We're using plastic 'cause we don't have glass." if
plastic_cup unless glass_cup
```

This trick is a gorgeous way of expressing, *Do this only if* **a** *is true and* **b** *isn't true.*

Now that you've met **false**, I'm sure you can see what's on next.

True

```
approaching_guy = true
```

I saw **true** at the hotel buffet tables today. I cannot stand that guy. His stance is way too wide. And you've never met anyone who planted his feet so hard in the ground. He wears this corny necklace made out of shells. His face exudes this brash confidence. (You can tell he's exerting all of his restraint just to keep from bursting into Neo flight.)

To be honest, I can't be around someone who always has to be right. This **true** is always saying, "A-OK." Flashing hang ten. And seriously, he loves that necklace. Wears it constantly.

As you'd suspect, he's backstage at everything on the **if** event schedule.

print "Hugo Boss" if true acts like **print "Hugo Boss"**.

Occasionally, **if** will haul out the velvet ropes to exercise some crowd control. The **double equals** gives the appearance of a short link of ropes, right along the sides of a red carpet where only **true** can be admitted.

Make Your Own Starmonkey!

1 Turn a mug upside-down.

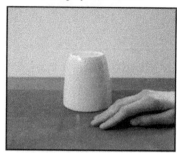

3 Shove car keys into the sides of the apple.

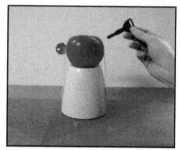

2 Attach an apple with a rubber band.

4 Glue star face.

You have two complementary star faces waiting in your account.

Standard, placid.   Eating chalk.

```
if approaching_guy == true
  print "That necklace is classic."
end
```

The double equals is simply **an ID check**. Do the gentleman at both ends of this rope appear to match?

In this way, you control who **if** lets in. If you have a hard time getting along with **true** as I do, you can heartily welcome **false**.

```
if approaching_guy == false
  print "Get in here, you conniving devil."
end
```

Same goes for **unless**. The gateway is yours. Take possession of it.

Again, I Want You to Dominate

Now, you want a head trip? **The double equals sign is a method.** Can you guess how it works? Here, check it out with the dot and parens:

```
approaching_guy.==( true )
```

Ruby allows the shortcut, though. You can drop the dot and back away slowly.

Now, do you remember what you need to do to **dominate** in Ruby? *Use the answers the methods give you.*

```
if nil.==( true )
  print "This will never see realization."
end
```

In the above, how is the method's answer being used?

Let's take the statement **nil.==(true)**. This will fail every time. No match. When there's no match, the double equals method answers with **false**. A shake of the head. That answer is given to **if**, who can't accept a **false**. The **print** never sees realization.

```
at_hotel = true
email = if at_hotel
          "why@hotelambrose.com"
       else
          "why@drnhowardcham.com"
       end
```

Even though **if** isn't a method, **if** does give a return answer. Look at the above and wonder over what happens when **at_hotel** is **true**.

The **if** will return the answer given by the code it chooses to run. In the case of **at_hotel** being true, the first string, my e-mail address at Hotel Ambrose, will be returned. The **else** keyword marks code which will run, should **if** fail. If **at_hotel** is false, the **if** will answer with my e-mail address at Dr. N. Howard Cham's office, where I take my apprenticeship.

Should you have several lines of code in an **if** or **unless**, **only the answer from the last full statement will be used**.

```
email = if at_hotel
          address = "why"
          address << "@hotelambrose"
          address << ".com"
       end
```

Three lines of code inside the **if**. The first line assigns a string with my name in it to a variable. The second and third lines add the rest of my e-mail address on to the end. The **double less-than << is the concatenation operator**. To concatenate is to **append**, or **add to the end**.

Just as we saw with the equality checker **==**, the concatenator is a method. After adding to the end of the string, the concatenator also **answers with that very string**. So, the third line, which could be read as **address.<<(".com")**, gives back **address**, which the **if** then hands back for **email**'s assignment.

Here's a question: what if the **if** fails? What if **at_hotel** is false in the above example? Is anything returned? Nothing is assigned to **email**, right?

Yes, nothing is returned. By which I mean: **nil** is returned. And often **nil** is a very useful answer.

```
print( if at_hotel.nil?
          "No clue if he's in the hotel."
      elsif at_hotel == true
          "Definitely in."
      elsif at_hotel == false
          "He's out."
      else
          "The system is on the freee-itz."
      end )
```

You can use the **nil?** method on any value in Ruby. Again, think of it as a message. To the value: "Are you nil? Are you empty?"

If **at_hotel** is empty, Ruby doesn't have any idea if I'm in the hotel or not. So **if** answers with the "No clue" string. In order to handle the **true** or **false** possibilities, the **elsif** keyword is used. While you can have only one **if** and one **else**, you can fill the in-between with an exorbitant number of **elsif** keywords. Each **elsif** acts as **a further if test**. Checking for a positive charge.

If you're doing okay at this point, then you're in tip-top shape for the rest of the book. You have seen some pretty tough code in the last few examples. You strong fellow.

3. Chaining Delusions Together

55,000 starmonkeys and one spirited Olympic hopeful.

You finish reading the above comic and retire to your daybed for reflection. It's one of those canopy affairs which is always logjammed with pillows. You sit atop the pile, gazing out upon the world. You see the tall smokestacks belching wide spools of fume and haze. The tangled concourses of freeways smattered with swift, shimmering traffic is but a gently pulsing eye muscle from your vantage point.

It is all so fantastic. How the colors of the horizon spread across the landscape as a great mix of butter and grease with a tablespoon of vanilla extract.

Yet, for all of the beauty which beckons for your attention, the images of the Elf and his Olympic Hopeful return. And more especially, that order for **55,000** starmonkeys. *55,000 starmonkeys*, you think. *Fifty-five Thousand.*

You think of just the number itself. *55,000*. It's walking down a road. It might be in a forest, you don't know for sure as your eyes are fixed right on the number itself. It's stopping and talking to people. To tennis players, to a men's choral group. There is merriment and good feeling. When it laughs, its lower zeros quiver with glee.

You want to talk to it. You want to skip along that forest trail with it. You want to climb aboard a jet bound to Brazil with it. And after five days and four nights at the leisureful Costa do Sauipe Marriott Resort & Spa, to marry it, to bear a family of 55,000 starmonkeys with it. To take possession of Nigeria with it.

With a flying leap, you dismount your pillow tower of isolation. Scrambling with the key, you unlock your roll top desk and pull out a sheet of paper, holding it firmly upon the desk. You begin scribbling.

> *Take possession of Nigeria with my new 55,000 starmonkeys... Over it, build Nigeria-sized **vegetarians only** casino and go-cart arena... Wings... we could have our own special sauce on the wings that's different... Mustard + codeine = Smotchkkiss' Starry Starmonkey Glow Sauce... Franchise, franchise... logos... Employee instructional videos... When you give the customer change, let them reach inside the frog on your hand to get it... If they have no change, at least put their reciept some place where they have to touch the frog... We're leveling the playing field here... Advertise cheap pizza, let's make our money off soda... Collect all 4 frosted glasses...*

Wow, the ideas are really coming out. You literally had to smack yourself to stop. We need to put these in a safe place. Actually, we should store them on your computer and mangle the words. You look out the window and watch for FBI. I'm going to start this script.

The Flipping Script

```
print "Type and be diabolical: "
idea_backwards = gets.reverse
```

Let this script be your confidante. It will ask for evil plans and turn their letters backwards. The **gets** method is **built into Ruby**. It's a **kernel method** like **print**. This method **gets** will pause Ruby to let you type. When you hit *Enter*, **gets** will then stop paying attention to your keyboard punchings and answer back to Ruby with a string that contains everything you typed.

The **reverse** method is then used on the string that **gets** is giving back. The **reverse** method is part of the **String** class. Which means that **anything which is a string has the reverse method available**. More on classes in the next chapter, for now just know that **a lot of methods are only available with certain types of values.**

I don't think **reverse** is going to cut it. The authorities only need to put a mirror to "airegiN fo noissessop ekaT." Bust us when starmonkeys start to touch down in Lagos.

The capital letters give it away. Maybe if we uppercase all letters in the string before we reverse it.

```
idea_backwards = gets.upcase.reverse
```

Your Repetitiveness Pays Off

You hand me a legal pad, doused in illegible shorthand. Scanning over it, I start to notice patterns. That you seem to use the same set of words repeatedly in your musings. Words like *starmonkey, Nigeria, firebomb*. Some phrases even. *Put the kibosh on*. That gets said a lot.

Let us disguise these foul terms, my brother. Let us obscure them from itching eyes that cry to know our delicate schemes and to thwart us from having great pleasure and many go-carts. We will replace them with the most innocent language. New words with secret meaning.

I start up a word list, a Ruby **Hash**, which contains these oft seen and dangerous words of yours. In the Hash, each dangerous word is matched up against a code word (or phrase). The code word will be swapped in for the real word.

```
CODE_WORDS = {
  'starmonkeys' => 'Phil and Pete, those prickly chancellors
of the New Reich',
  'catapult' => 'chucky go-go',
  'firebomb' => 'Heat-Assisted Living',
  'Nigeria' => "Ny and Jerry's Dry Cleaning (with Donuts)",
  'Put the kibosh on' => 'Put the cable box on'
}
```

The words which are placed before the arrow are called **keys**. The words after the arrows, the definitions, are often just called **values**.

Notice the double quotes around `Ny and Jerry's Dry Cleaning (with Donuts)`. Since a single quote is being used as an apostrophe, we can't use single quotes around the string. (Although, you can use single quotes if you put a backslash before the apostrophe such as: `'Ny and Jerry\'s Dry Cleaning (with Donuts)'`.)

Should you need to look up a specific word, you can do so by using the **square brackets** method.

`CODE_WORDS['catapult']` will answer with the string `'chucky go-go'`.

Look at the square brackets as if they are a wooden pallet the word is sitting upon. A forklift could slide its prongs into each side of the pallet and bring it down from a shelf back in the warehouse. The word on the pallet is called the *index*. We are asking the forklift to find the index for us and bring back its corresponding value.

If you've never been to a warehouse, you could also look at the brackets as handles. Imagine an industrious worker putting on his work gloves and hefting the index back to your custody. If you've never used handles before, then I'm giving you about thirty seconds to find a handle and use it before I blow my lid.

As with many of the other operators you've seen recently, the index brackets are simply a shortcut for a method.

`CODE_WORDS.[]( 'catapult' )` will answer with the string `'chucky go-go'`.[4]

---

4 Publisher's note: *CODE_WORDS* is not a constant in the Wayback Machine version.

Get Ahead with The Tiger's Vest

Want to start using Ruby alongside your reading? Split your attention and head off to Expansion Pak I: The Tiger's Vest, a trite mini-chapter which will aid you in installing Ruby. In addition, you'll learn how to use Irb and Ri, two teaching aids that come with Ruby which will really speed you up in your learning.[3]

---

3 Publisher's note: Read the archived Expansion Pak at https://poignant.guide/book/expansion-pak-1.html. It's a little out of date, and deals with the set up of supporting Ruby tools like **irb** and **ri**.

Making the Swap

I went ahead and saved the Hash of code words to a file called **wordlist.rb**

```ruby
require_relative 'wordlist'5

# Get evil idea and swap in code words
print "Enter your new idea: "
idea = gets
CODE_WORDS.each do |real, code|
  idea.gsub!( real, code )
end


# Save the jibberish to a new file
print "File encoded.  Please enter a name for this idea: "
idea_name = gets.strip
File::open( "idea-" + idea_name + ".txt", "w" ) do |f|
  f << idea
end
```

Script starts by pulling in our word list. Like **gets** and **print**, the **require_relative** method is a kernel method, you can use it anywhere. I give it the string **'wordlist'** and it will look for a file named **wordlist.rb**.

After that, there are two sections. I am marking these sections with comments, the lines that start with **pound** symbols. Comments are **useful notes** that accompany your code. Folks who come wandering through your code will appreciate the help. When going through your own code after some time has passed, comments will help you get back into your mindset. And there's software out there that can take your comments and build documents from them. (RDoc and Ri—see Expansion Pak #1![6])

I like comments because I can skim a big pile of code and spot the highlights.

As the comments tell us, the first section asks you for your evil idea and swaps in the new code words. The second section saves the encoded idea into a new text file.

---

5 Publisher's note: *require_relative* was *require* in the Wayback Machine version.
6 Publisher's note: Read the archived Expansion Pak at https://poignant.guide/book/expansion-pak-1.html.

```
CODE_WORDS.each do |real, code|
  idea.gsub!( real, code )
end
```

You see the **each** method? The **each** method is all over in Ruby. It's available for Arrays, Hashes, even Strings. Here, our **CODE_WORDS** dictionary is kept in a Hash. This **each** method will hurry through **all the pairs of the Hash,** one dangerous word matched with its code word, handing each pair to the **gsub!** method for the actual replacement.

In Ruby, **gsub** is short for *global substitution*. The method is used to search and replace. Here, we want to find all the occurrences of a dangerous word and replace with its safe code word. With **gsub,** you provide the **word to find as the first argument,** then the **word to put in its place as the second argument**.

Why aren't we hanging on to the answer from **gsub**? Doesn't **gsub** give us an answer back that we should keep? You'd think the line would read:

```
safe_idea = idea.gsub( real, code )
```

Yes, with **gsub** we'd need to hang on to its answer. We're using a variation of **gsub** that is totally hyper. Notice the **exclamation mark** on the **gsub!** used inside the **each** block. The exclamation mark is a sign that **gsub!** is a bit of a zealot. See, **gsub!** will go ahead and **replace the words in `idea` directly**. When it's done `idea` will contain the newly altered string and you won't be able to find the old string.

Call **gsub!** a **destructive method**. It makes its changes to the value directly. Whereas **gsub** will leave the value intact, answering back with a new string which contains the alterations. (Why must **gsub!** scream when he descends upon his prey? Merciless assailant!)

Text Files of a Madman

Let us now save the encoded idea to a file.

```ruby
# Save the jibberish to a new file
print "File encoded.  Please enter a name for this idea: "
idea_name = gets.strip
File::open( 'idea-' + idea_name + '.txt', 'w' ) do |f|
  f << idea
end
```

This section starts by asking you for a name by which the idea can be called. This name is used to build a file name when we save the idea.

The **strip** method is for strings. This method **trims spaces and blank lines** from the **beginning and end** of the string. This will remove the *Enter* at the end of the string you typed. But it'll also handle spaces if you accidentally left any.

After we have the idea's name, we open a new, blank text file. The file name is built by adding strings together. If you typed in **'mustard-plus-codeine'**, then our math will be: **'idea-'** + **'mustard-plus-codeine'** + **'.txt'**. Ruby presses these into a single string. **'idea-mustard-plus-codeine.txt'** is the file.

We're using the class method **File::open** to create the new file. Up until now, we've used several kernel methods to do our work. We hand the **print** method a string and it prints the string on your screen. One secret about kernel methods like **print**: they are actually **class methods**.

```ruby
Kernel::print( "55,000 Starmonkey Salute!" )
```

What does this mean? Why does it matter? It means **Kernel** is the center of Ruby's universe. Wherever you are in your script, **Kernel** is right beside you. You don't even need to spell **Kernel** out for Ruby. Ruby knows to check **Kernel**.

Most methods are more specialized than **print** or **gets**. Take the **File::open** for example. The creator of Ruby, Matz, has given us many different methods which read, rename, or delete files. They are all organized inside the **File** class.

- **File::read("idea-mustard-plus-codeine.txt")** will answer back with a string containing all of the text from your idea file.

- **File::rename("old_file.txt", "new_file.txt")** will rename **old_file.txt**.

- **File::delete("new_file.txt")** will nuke the new file.

These File methods are all **built right into Ruby**. They are all just stored in a container called the **File** class. So, while you can safely call kernel methods without needing to type **Kernel**, Ruby doesn't automatically check the **File** class. You'll need to give the full method name.

```
File::open( 'idea-' + idea_name + '.txt', 'w' ) do |f|
  f << idea
end
```

We pass two arguments into **File::open**. The first is the **file name to open**. The second is a string containing our **file mode**. We use **'w'**, which means to write to a brand-new file. (Other options are: **'r'** to read from the file or **'a'** to add to the end of the file.)

The file is opened for writing and we are handed back the file in variable **f**, which can be seen **sliding down the chute into our block**. Inside the block, we write to the file. When the block closes with **end**, our file is closed as well.

Notice we use the **concatenator <<** to write to the file. We can do this because files have a method called **<<** just like strings do.

Settle Down, Your Ideas Aren't Trapped

Here, let's get your ideas back to their original verbage, so you can ruminate over their brilliance.

```ruby
require_relative 'wordlist'

# Print each idea out with the words fixed
Dir['idea-*.txt'].each do |file_name|
  idea = File.read( file_name )
  CODE_WORDS.each do |real, code|
    idea.gsub!( code, real )
  end
  puts idea
end
```

By now, you should be up to snuff with most of this example. I won't bore you with all of the mundane details. See if you can figure out how it works on your own.

We have an interesting class method here, though. The **Dir::[]** method searches a directory (some of you may call them "folders"). Just as you've seen with Hashes, the index brackets can be class methods. (Can you start to see the shiny, glinting gorgeousness of Ruby?)

So we're using the forklift to get those files in the directory which match **'idea-*.txt'**. The **Dir::[]** method will use the asterisk as a wildcard. We're basically saying, "Match anything that starts with *idea-* and ends with *.txt.*" The forklift shuffles off to the directory and comes back with a list of all matching files.

That **list of files** will come in the form of **Array** the Caterpillar, with a **String** for each file. If you are curious and want to play with **Dir::[]**, try this:

```ruby
p Dir['idea-*.txt']
#=> ['idea-mustard-plus-codeine.txt'] # an Array of file
names!
```

Yes, the **p** method works like **print**. But where **print** is designed for displaying strings, **p** will print *anything*. Check this out.

```ruby
p File::methods
#=> ["send", "display", "name", "exist?", "split", ...]
# a whole list of method names!
```

4. The Miracle of Blocks

Flowerboyz? Heard it before.

Since you and I are becoming closer friends as we share this time together, I should probably let you in on a bit of the history going on here. It's a good time for a break I say.

First, you should know that Blix is my cat. My second pet to Bigelow. Granted, we hardly see each other anymore. He's completely self-sufficient. I'm not exactly sure where he's living these days, but he no longer lives in the antechamber to my quarters. He emptied his savings account about seven months ago.

He does have a set of keys for the house and the Seville. Should he ever find himself stranded, I will gladly step away from our differences and entertain his antics around the house again.

Make no mistake. I miss having him around. Can't imagine he misses my company, but I miss his.

A Siren and A Prayer

I first saw Blix on television when I was a boy. He had a starring role on a

Excerpt from The Scarf Eaters
(from Chapter V: A Man in Uniform.)

In April, the callow lilies came back. They stretched their baby angel wings out and reached for the world. Gently, their tendrils caressed the sullen fence posts until even they lilted lovelier.

From her bedroom window, Lara watched the lilies exude their staunch femininity. She slipped the tassels of a fresh, carpathian, embroidered scarf into her mouth and ate slowly. The long cloth slid down her throat and tickled as it snaked along her esophagus. She giggled and burped.

Oh, how the flora drew her in. Looking at flowers went so well with being a teenage girl. She wanted to paint them, so she opened a new Flash template. A blank movie this time.

She set her cursor loose in the garden of her movie's viewable area. Vector white lines below shorter vector yellow lines. She selected the white lines and grouped them together. She even moved them to a new layer entitled "Cry, Baby Angel, Cry." Then she converted them into a graphic object and moved them to the library.

She felt a warm chill as she moved the long, white petals to her movie's library. It felt so official. **I choose you. I name you. Dwell in the comfort of my palace forevermore.**

Heh. She laughed. Colorado Springs was hardly a "palace."

Since they had moved, Dad had only been home once. He had barged through the front door in full uniform and had given quite a start to both Lara and her mother. Her mother had even dropped a head of lettuce—which head she had just finished washing—in a pitcher of Lick-M-Aid.

The pitcher was just wide enough for the lettuce and it lodged in there pretty good. Dad came over and yanked at the moist head for sometime until declaring it FUBAR, in a voice both bemused and then crestfallen. He tossed the clotted spout in the trash bin.

It was only later that day that Lara's mother realized that she could have simply halved the lettuce with an electric knife. Dad laughed and slapped his forehead. He then went around and slapped Lara's forehead, and her mother's too, affectionately.

"We just weren't thinking, were we?" is what he said. "And who dares blame us? We're a real family today. And we shouldn't have to do anything else on the day we got our family back."

Lara's smiled reflected across the glass of her monitor. She chose the text tool and in 42 point serif typed: "Dad." She created a path for it and let it tween off the right side of the screen. She cried long after it was gone.

very gritty police drama called *A Siren and A Prayer*. The show was about a god-fearing police squad that did their jobs, did them well, and saw their share of miracles out on the beat. I mean the officers on this show were *great* guys, very religious, practically clergy. But, you know, even clergymen don't have the good sense to kill a guy after he's gone too far. These guys knew where to draw that line. They walked that line every day.

So, it was a pretty bloody show, but they always had a good moral at the end. Most times the moral was something along the lines of, "Wow, we got out of that one quick." But there's serious camaraderie in a statement like that.

The show basically revolved around this one officer. "Mad" Dick Robinson. People called him Mad because he was basically insane. I can't remember if he was actually clinically insane, but people were always questioning his decisions. Mad often blew his top and chewed out some of the other officers, most of whom had unquestionable moral character. But we all know it's a tough world, the stakes are high out there, and everyone who watched the show held Mad in great regard. I think everyone on the squad grew quite a bit as people, thanks to Mad's passion.

The officers couldn't do it all themselves though. In every single episode, they plead with a greater force for assistance. And, in every single episode, they got their tips from a cat named Terry (played by my cat Blix.) He was just a kitten at the time and, as a young boy tuning into *A Siren and A Prayer*, I found myself longing for my own crime-sniffing cat. Terry took these guys down the subway tunnels, through the rotting stench of abandoned marinas, into backdoors of tall, industrial smokestacks.

Sometimes he was all over an episode, darting in and out, preparing traps and directing traffic. But other times you wouldn't see him the whole episode. Then you'd rewind through the whole show and look and look and look. You'd give up. He can't be in that episode.

Still, you can't bear to let it go, so you go comb through the whole episode with the jog on your remote, combing, pouring over each scene. And there he is. Way up behind the floodlight that was turned up too high. The one that left Mad with permanent eye damage. Why? Why burn out the retinas of your own colleague, Terry?

But the question never got answered because the series was cancelled. They started to do special effects with the cat and it all fell apart. In the last episode of the show, there is a moment where Terry is trapped at the top of a crane, about to fall into the searing slag in the furnace of an iron smelt. He looks back. No going back. He looks down. Paws over eyes (*no joke!*), he leaps from the crane and, mid-flight, snags a rope and swings to safety, coming down on a soft antelope hide that one of the workers had presumably been tanning that afternoon.

People switched off the television set the very moment the scene aired. They tried changing the name. First it was *God Gave Us a Squad. Kiss of Pain.* Then, *Kiss of Pain in Maine,* since the entire precinct ended up relocating there. But the magic was gone. I went back to summer school that year to make up some classes and all the kids had pretty much moved on to football pencils.

Blocks

A couple years ago, I started teaching Blix about Ruby. When we got to this part in his lessons, the part that covers blocks, he said to me, "Blocks remind me of Mad Dick Robinson."

"Oh?" I hadn't heard that name in awhile. "I can't see how that could be."

"Well, you say blocks can be difficult to understand."

"They're not difficult," I said. "A **block** is just **code that's grouped together.**"

"And Mad was just an officer, sworn to uphold his duty," he said. "But he was a real miracle to watch out in the field. Now, this first example you've shown me..." He pointed to an example I'd written down for him.

```
kitty_toys =
  [:shape => 'sock', :fabric => 'cashmere'] +
  [:shape => 'mouse', :fabric => 'calico'] +
  [:shape => 'eggroll', :fabric => 'chenille']
kitty_toys.sort_by { |toy| toy[:fabric] }
```

"This is a small miracle," he said. "I can't deny its beauty. Look, there are my kitty toys, laid out with their characteristics. Below them, the block, sorting them by fabric."

"I apologize if your list of toys looks a bit tricky," I said. Like you, he had learned about the Array, the caterpillar stapled into the code, with square brackets on each side and each item separated by commas. (Ah, here is one: **['sock', 'mouse', 'eggroll']**.) He had also been taught the Hash, which is like a dictionary, with curly braces on each end which look like small, open books. Commas in the Hash between each pair. Each word in the dictionary matched up with its definition by an arrow. (Be beholden: **{'blix' => 'cat', 'why' => 'human'}**.)

"Yes, vexing," he said. "It has square brackets like it's an Array, but with the arrows like it's a Hash. I don't think you're going to get away with that."

"It does seem a bit subversive, doesn't it?" I said, tease-nudging him with a spoon. "I've done your kitty toy list in a mix of the two. I'm using a shortcut. Which is: **If you use arrows inside of an Array, you'll end up with a Hash inside of that Array.**"

"Oh, I see," he said. "You criss-crossed 'em. How neat!"

"Yes, yes, you're on it," I said. He was also very good with a protractor. "I have three Arrays, each with a Hash inside. Notice the plus signs? I'm adding them into one big Array. Here's another way of writing it..." I jotted down.

```
kitty_toys = [
  {:shape => 'sock', :fabric => 'cashmere'},
  {:shape => 'mouse', :fabric => 'calico'},
  {:shape => 'eggroll', :fabric => 'chenille'}
]
```

One Array, which acts as our list of chew toys. Three Hashes in the Array to describe each toy.

Sorting and Iterating to Save Lives

"Let's sort your toys by shape now," I said. "Then, we'll print them out in that order."

```
kitty_toys.sort_by { |toy| toy[:shape] }.each do |toy|
  puts "Blixy has a #{ toy[:shape] } made of #{ toy[:fabric] }"
end
```

"How does **sort_by** work?" asked Blix. "I can tell it's a method you can use with Arrays. Because **kitty_toys** is an Array. But what is **toy**?"

"Okay, **toy** is a **block argument**," I said. "Remember: the skinny pipes on each side of **toy** make it a **chute**."

"Sure, but it looks like you're using it like a Hash. Inside the block you have **toy[:shape]**. That looks like a Hash."

"The **sort_by** method is an **iterator**, Blix. It **iterates**, or **cycles**, through **a list of things**. You remember that episode when Mad..."

"Episode?" he said. Yeah, he can't understand the concept of TV dramas. Yeah, I've tried explaining.

"Or, yeah, remember that one *eyewitness account* we watched where Mad was trying to talk down that crazy spelling bee contestant from the ledge of an college library?"

"I remember it better than you because I was riding in a remote control plane." Yep, it was one of those episodes.

"Do you remember how Mad got the guy to come down?" I asked.

"People in spelling bees love letters," said Blix. "So what Mad did was a genius move on his part. He started with the letter A and gave reasons, for all the letters of the alphabet, why the guy should walk back down the building and be safe on the ground."

"'A is for the Architecture of buildings like this,'" I said, in a gruff Mad voice. "'Which give us hope in a crumbling world.'"

"'B is for Big Guys, like your friend Mad the Cop,'" said Blix. "'Guys who help people all the time and don't know how to spell too great, but still help guys who spell really great.'"

"See, he went through all the letters, one at a time. He was *iterating* through them." *It Err Ate Ing.*

"But the guy jumped anyway, Why. He jumped off on letter Q or something."

"'Q is for Quiet Moments that help us calm down and think about all of life's little pleasures, so we don't get all uptight and starting goofing around on tiptoes at the very edge of a big, bad building.'"

"And then he jumped," said Blix. He shook his head. "You can't blame Mad. He did his best."

"He had a big heart, that's for sure," I said, patting Blix on the shoulder.

```
kitty_toys.sort_by { |toy| toy[:shape] }.each do |toy|
  puts "Blixy has a #{ toy[:shape] } made of #{ toy[:fabric] }"
end
```

"As for your **sort_by**, it **starts at the top** of the list and **goes through each item**, one at a time. So **toy** is one of those items. With each item, **sort_by** stops and **slides that item down the chute**, under the **toy** name, and lets you figure out what to do with it."

"Okay, so **toy** takes turns being each of the different toys I have."

"That's right," I said. "You know how I've really been harping on *using the answers that methods give you*? Here, we're simply looking up the toy's shape inside the block. The block then answers to **sort_by** with the shape string, such as **"mouse"** or **"sock"**. Once it's done cycling through the whole list, **sort_by** will have alphabetically compared each of the shape strings and will give back a new sorted Array."

An Unfinished Lesson

"That's good enough for today," said Blix. "Can I have a fresh saucer of milk, please?"

I filled his saucer to the brim and he guzzled from it for some time while I took a poker and jabbed at coals in the fireplace. My mind wandered and I couldn't help but think further of blocks. I wondered what I would teach Blix next.

I probably would have taught him about **next**. When you are iterating through a list, you may use **next** to **skip on to the next item**. Here we're counting toys that have a non-eggroll shape by skipping those that do with **next**.

```ruby
non_eggroll = 0
kitty_toys.each do |toy|
  next if toy[:shape] == 'eggroll'
  non_eggroll = non_eggroll + 1
end
```

I could also have taught him about **break**, which **kicks you out of an iterating loop**. In the code below, we'll print out (with **p**) each of the toy Hashes until we hit the toy whose fabric is chenille. The **break** will cause the **each** to abruptly end.

```ruby
kitty_toys.each do |toy|
  break if toy[:fabric] == 'chenille'
  p toy
end
```

I never got to teach him such things. I continued poking away at a particularly stubborn coal which was caught in the iron curtain of the fireplace and threatened to drop on my antelope skin rug.

As I hacked away ferociously at the black stone, Blix slipped away, presumably on the bus bound for Wixl, the very bustling metropolis of the animal economies. Who knows, he may have first stopped in Ambrose or Riathna or any of the other villages along the way. My instinct says that Wixl was definitely his final stop.

Without any student to instruct and coax along, I found myself quite lonely, holed up in the estate. In the stillness of the dead corridors, I began to sketch out a biography in the form of this guide.

I worked on it whenever I found myself bored. And when I wasn't bored, I could always switch on *The Phantom Menace* to get me in the mood.

Someone let them all out.

Through space and time... in his bell jar... on a mission to find himself...

Them What Make the Rules and Them What Live the Dream

Frankly, I'm sick and tired of hearing that Dr. Cham was a madman. Yes, he tried to bury himself alive. Yes, he electrocuted his niece. Yes, in fact, he did dynamite a retirement home. But this was all with good cause and, in each case, I believe he took the correct course of action.

I'm sure you'd like to side with popular opinion, but you're bound to feel some small trickle of admiration for him once he's taken time to teach you all about Ruby's class definitions. And moreso when you learn about mixins. And perhaps, by the end of the chapter, we can all start to look beyond the Doctor's grievous past and stop calling him a madman.

So if you need to call him a madman, I'd start heading down to the train tracks to smash up some long fluorescent light bulbs. Get it out of your system right now, before we dig in.

1. This One's For the Disenfranchised

Some people still can't get past what he did.

If you give me a number, which is any year from Dr. Cham's life, I'll give you a synopsis of that time period. And I'll do it as a Ruby method, so it's an independent piece, an isolated chunk of code which can be hooked up to the voice of a robotic volcano, when such a thing becomes the apex of authoritative voice talents.

Okay, so I need you to notice **def** and **case** and **when**. You've seen the Ranges, the closed accordions of **1895..1913**, back in chapter 3. They contain both ends and in between. And the backslashes at the end of each line simply ignore the *Enter* key at the end of each line, assuring Ruby that there is *more of this line to come*.

So, please: **def** and **case** and **when**.

```ruby
def dr_chams_timeline( year )
  case year
  when 1894
    "Born."
  when 1895..1913
    "Childhood in Lousville, Winston Co., Mississippi."
  when 1914..1919
    "Worked at a pecan nursery; punched a Quaker."
  when 1920..1928
    "Sailed in the Brotherhood of River Wisdomming, \
    which journeyed the Mississippi River and engaged \
    in thoughtful self-improvement, where he \
    finished 140 credit hours from their Oarniversity."
  when 1929
    "Returned to Louisville to pen a novel about \
    time-travelling pheasant hunters."
  when 1930..1933
    "Took up a respectable career insuring pecan \
    nurseries.  Financially stable, he spent \
    time in Brazil and New Mexico, buying up \
    rare paper-shell pecan trees.  Just as his \
    notoriety came to a crescendo: gosh, he tried \
    to buried himself alive."
  when 1934
    "Went back to writing his novel.  Changed the \
    hunters to insurance tycoons and the pheasants \
    to Quakers."
  when 1935..1940
    "Took Arthur Cone, the Headmaster of the \
    Brotherhood of River Wisdomming, \
    as a houseguest.  Together for five years, \
    engineering and inventing."
  when 1941
    "And this is where things got interesting."
  end
end
```

The **def** keyword. Here is our first **method definition**. A plain kernel method, which can be used anywhere in Ruby. And how do we run it?

```
puts dr_chams_timeline( 1941 )
```

Which answers with "And this is where things got interesting." It's the same story again and again: *use your answers*. I've set things up above so that the **case** statement always answers with a string. And since the case statement is the final (and only) statement in the method, then the method answers with that string. Trickling water spilling down from ledge to ledge.

Let me be clear about the **case** statement. Actually, I should call it a **case..when** statement, since they cannot be used separately. The **case** keyword is followed by a value, which is compared against each of the values which follow **when** keywords. The first value to qualify as a match is the one the case uses and the rest are ignored. You can do the same thing with a bunch of **if..elsif** statements, but it's wordier.

```
case year
when 1894
  "Born."
when 1895..1913
  "Childhood in Lousville, Winston Co., Mississippi."
else
  "No information about this year."
end
```

Is identical to:

```
if 1894 === year
  "Born."
elsif (1895..1913) === year
  "Childhood in Lousville, Winston Co., Mississippi."
else
  "No information about this year."
end
```

The **triple equals** is a length of velvet rope, checking values much like the double equals. It's just: the triple equals is a longer rope and it sags a bit in the middle. It's not as strict, it's a bit more flexible.

Take the Ranges above. **(1895..1913)** isn't at all **equal** to **1905**. No, the Range **(1895..1913)** is only truly **equal** to any other Range **(1895..1913)**. In the case of a Range, the triple equals cuts you a break and lets the Integer **1905** in, because even though it's not **equal** to the Range, it's **included** in the set of Integers represented by the Range. Which is good enough in some cases, such as the timeline I put together earlier.

Which actually looked like a timeline, didn't it? I mean, sure, `dr_chams_timeline` method is code, but it does read like a timeline, clean and lovely.

What research revealed.

But Was He Sick??

You know, he had such bad timing. He was scattered as a novelist, but his ventures into alchemy were very promising. He had an elixir of goat's milk and sea salt that got rid of leg aches. One guy even grew an inch on a thumb he'd lost. He had an organic health smoke that smelled like foot but gave you night vision. He was working on something called Liquid Ladder, but I've never seen or read anything else about it. It can't have been for climbing. Who knows.

Caring For You. And Your Wellness.

I need you to be in a good mental state for the latter half of this book. Now is the time to begin conditioning you.

Let's start with some deep breathing. Give me a good deep breath and count to four with me.

Here we go. 1. 2. 3. 4. Now exhale. You can feel your eyes. Good, that's exactly it.

Now let's take a deep breath and, in your mind, draw a hippopotamus as fast as you can. Quick quick. His legs, his folds, his marshmallow teeth. Okay, done. Now exhale.

Take another deep breath and hold it tight. As you hold it tightly in your chest, imagine the tightness is shrinking you down into a bug. You've held your breath so hard that you're an insect. And all the other bugs saw you shrink and they loved the stunt. They're clapping and rubbing their feelers together madly. But you had an apple in your hand when you were big and it just caught up with you, crushed the whole crowd. You're dead, too. Now exhale.

Give me a solid deep breath and imagine you live in a town where everything is made of telephone cords. The houses are all telephone cords, the shingles, the rafters. The doorways are a thick mass of telephone cords which you simply thrust yourself through.

When you go to bed, the bedspread is telephone cords. And the mattress and box springs are telephone cords, too. Like I said, everything is made out of telephone cords. The telephone itself is made of telephone cords. But the telephone cord going to the telephone is made out of bread and a couple sticks. Now exhale.

Breathe in. 1. 2. 3. 4. Breathe out.

Breath in. 1. 2. Another short breath in. 3. 4. Imagine both of your hands snapping off at the wrists and flying into your computer screen and programming it from the inside. Exhale.

Big, big deep breath. Deep down inside you there is a submarine. It has a tongue. Exhale.

*Breathe through your nostrils. Deep breath. Filter the air through your nostrils. Breathing through the nostrils gives you quality air. Your nostrils flare, you are taking breaths of nature's air, the way God intended. Imagine a floppy disk drive clogged up with orphans. And while it chokes on orphans, you have good, wholesome God's breath in your lungs. But that pleasurable, life-giving air will become a powerful toxin if held too long. **Hurry, exhale God and nature's air!***

Now, you will wake up, smoothing out the creases of this page in your web browser. You will have full recollection of your whole life and not forgetting any one of the many adventures you have had in your life. You will feel rich and renewed and expert. You will have no remembrance of this short exercise, you will instead remember teaching a rabbit to use scissors from a great distance.

*And as you will wake up with your eyes directed to the top of this exercise, you will begin again. But this time, try to imagine that even **your shadow** is a telephone cord.*

One local newspaper actually visited Dr. Cham. Their book reviewer gave him four stars. Really. She did an article on him. Gave him a rating.

Just know that Dr. N. Harold Cham felt terrible about his niece. He felt the shock treatment would work. The polio probably would have killed her anyway, but he took the chance.

On Sept. 9, 1941, after sedating her with a dose of phenacetin in his private operating room,

he attached the conducting clips to Hannah's nose, tongue, toes, and elbows. Assisted by his apprentice, a bespeckled undergraduate named Marvin Holyoake, they sprinkled the girl with the flakes of a substance the doctor called *opus magnum*. A white powder gold which would carry the current and blatantly energize the girl, forcing her blood to bloom and fight and vanquish.

But how it failed, oh, and how, when the lever was tossed, she arched and kicked—and **KABLAM!**—and **BLOY-OY-OY-KKPOY!** Ringlets of hair and a wall of light, and the bell of death rang. The experiment collapsed in a dire plume of smoke and her innocence (*for weeks, everyone started out with, "And she will never have the chance..."*) was a great pit in the floor and in their lungs.

To Hannah, I code.

```
opus_magnum = true
def save_hannah
  success = opus_magnum
end
```

A method is its own island. And what goes on inside is unaffected by the simple variables around it. Dr. Cham couldn't breach the illness of his niece, no more than an **opus_magnum** variable can penetrate the steely exterior of a method.

Should we run the **save_hannah** method, Ruby will squawk at us, claiming it sees no **opus_magnum**.

I'm talking about **scope**. Microscopes narrow and magnify your vision. Telescopes extend the range of your vision. In Ruby, **scope** refers to a field of vision inside methods and blocks.

A method's **def** statement opens its vision. Variable names introduced there will be seen by the method and kept meaningful until its **end** closes its eyes. You can pass data into a method by using arguments and data can be returned from the method, but the names used inside the method are only good for its scope.

Some variables have wider scope. Global variables like **$LOAD_PATH**, which start with a **cash** symbol, are available in any scope. Instance variables like **@names**, which start with an **at** are available anywhere inside a class scope. Same goes for class variables like **@@tickets**. Class and instance variables will be explored in a moment.

Blocks have scope, but it's a bit fuzzier. More flexible.

```
verb = 'rescued'
['sedated', 'sprinkled', 'electrocuted'].each do |verb|
  puts "Dr. Cham " + verb + " his niece Hannah."
end
puts "Finally, Dr. Cham " + verb + " his niece Hannah."
```

The block *iterates* (spins, cycles) through each of the Doctor's actions. The **verb** variable changes with each pass. In one pass, he's sedating. In the next, he's powdering. Then, he's electrocuting.

So, the question is: after the block's over, will he have rescued Hannah?

```
Dr. Cham sedated his niece Hannah.
Dr. Cham sprinkled his niece Hannah.
Dr. Cham electrocuted his niece Hannah.
Finally, Dr. Cham rescued his niece Hannah.
```

Blocks are allowed to see variables in the vicinity. But this block has its own **verb** variable which is updated each cycle. When the block completed and its tiny life ended, the outer **verb** stayed the same as it was before.[7]

This is the nature of local variables. When its **scope** closes, the variable goes away with it. Say that **verb** wasn't used before the block.

```
['sedated', 'powdered', 'electrocuted'].each do |verb|
  puts "Dr. Cham " + verb + " his niece Hannah."
end
puts "Yes, Dr. Cham " + verb + " his niece Hannah."
```

Pulls an error: **undefined local variable or method `verb'**. Poof. The inner variable won't leak outside its scope.

It must be something difficult, even for a great scientist, to carry away the corpse of a young girl whose dress is still starched and embroidered, but whose mouth is darkly clotted purple at the corners. In Dr. Cham's journal, he writes that he was tormented

---

7 Publisher's note: we have used the edited version of this section that appears on https://poignant.guide. See the Wayback Machine for the original.

by her ghost, which glistened gold and scorched lace. His delusions grew and he ran from hellhounds and massive vengeful, angelic hands.

Only weeks later, he was gone, propelled from these regrets, vanishing in the explosion that lifted him from the planet.

And even as you are reading this now, sometime in these moments, the bell jar craft of our lone Dr. Cham touched down upon a distant planet after a sixty year burn. As the new world came into view, as the curvature of the planet widened, as the bell jar whisked through the upset heavens, tearing through sheets of aurora and solar wind, Dr. Cham's eyes were shaken open.

Safe landing. Amazement.

What you are witnessing is the landing of Dr. Cham on the planet Endertromb. From what I can gather, he landed during the cusp of the Desolate Season, a time when there really isn't much happening on the planet. Most of the inhabitants find their minds locked into a listless hum which causes them to disintegrate into just vapid ghosts of one-part-wisdom and three-parts-steam for a time.

My modest grasp of the history and climate of Endertromb has been assembled from hanging around my daughter's organ instructor, who grew up on the planet.

Dead husbands could destroy the Doctor.

I frequently drill my daughter's organ instructor in order to ensure that he can keep appointments adequately. That he can take house calls at odd hours and promptly answer emergency calls. When he finally revealed to me that he was an alien whose waking day consisted of five-hundred and forty waking hours, I was incredibly elated and opened a contractual relationship with him which will last into 2060.

For three days (by his pocket watch's account), Dr. Cham traveled the dark shafts of air, sucking the dusty wind of the barren planet. But on the third day, he found the Desolate Season ending and he awoke to a brilliant vista, decorated with spontaneous apple blossoms and dewy castle tiers.

2. A Castle Has Its Computers

The panoramic vales of Sedna on Endertromb.

Our intrepid Doctor set off for the alien castle, dashing through the flowers. The ground belted past his heels. The castle inched up the horizon. He desired a stallion, but no stallion appeared. And that's how he discovered that the planet wouldn't read his mind and answer his wishes.

As my daughter's organ instructor explained it, however, the planet **could read minds** and it **could grant wishes**. Just not both at the same time.

One day as I quizzed the organ maestro, he sketched out the following Ruby code on a pad of cheese-colored paper. (And queer cheese smells were coming from somewhere, I can't say where.

```ruby
require 'endertromb'
class WishMaker
  def initialize
    @energy = rand( 6 )
  end
  def grant( wish )
    if wish.length > 10 or wish.include? ' '
      raise ArgumentError, "Bad wish."
    end
    if @energy.zero?
      raise Exception, "No energy left."
    end
    @energy -= 1
    Endertromb::make( wish )
  end
end
```

This is the wish maker.

Actually, no, this is a **definition for a wish maker.** To Ruby, it's a **class definition**. The code describes how a certain **object** will work.

Each morning, the wish maker starts out with up to five wishes available for granting. A new **WishMaker** is created at sun up.

```ruby
todays_wishes = WishMaker.new
```

The **new** method is a class method which creates a new, blank object. It also calls the object's **initialize** method automatically. In the **WishMaker** definition, you'll see the **initialize** method, which contains a single line of code: **@energy = rand(6)**.

The **rand(6)** picks a number between 0 and 5. This number will represent the number of wishes left in the day. So, occasionally there are no wishes available from the wish maker.

The random number is assigned to an **instance variable** which is named **@energy**. This instance variable will be available any time throughout the class. The variable can't be used outside the **scope** of the class.

In chapter three, we briefly looked at instance variables and decided to respect them as **attributes**. (The **at symbol** could mean **attribute**.) Instance variables can be used to store any kind of information, but they're most often used to store bits of information about the object represented by the class.

In the above case, each wish maker for the day has its own energy level. If the wish maker were a machine, you might see a gauge on it that points to the energy left inside. The **@energy** instance variable is going to act as that gauge.

```
todays_wishes = WishMaker.new
todays_wishes.grant( "antlers" )
```

Okay, step back and ensure you understand the example here. The **WishMaker** class is an outline we've laid out for how the whole magic wish program works. It's not the *actual* genie in the bottle, it's the paperwork behind the scenes. It's the rules and obligations the genie has to live by.

It's **todays_wishes** that's the genie in the bottle. And here we're giving it a wish to grant. Give us antlers, genie. (If you really get antlers from this example, I don't want to hear about it. Go leap in meadows with your own kind now.)

In the last chapter, the drill was: Ruby has two halves.

1.   Defining things.
2.   Putting those things into action.

What are the actions in Ruby? Methods. And now, you're having a lick of the definition language built-in to Ruby. Method definitions using **def**. Class definitions using **class**.

At this point in your instruction, it's easier to understand that **everything in Ruby is an object.**

```
number = 5
print number.next                    # prints '6'

phrase = 'wishing for antlers'
print phrase.length                  # prints '19'

todays_wishes = WishMaker.new
todays_wishes.grant( "antlers" )
```

And, consequently, each object has a class behind the scenes.

```
print 5.class                       # prints 'Integer'
print 'wishing for antlers'.class   # prints 'String'
print WishMaker.new.class           # prints 'WishMaker'
```

Dr. Cham never saw the wish maker as he hustled across the landspace. It lay far beyond his landing in the valley of Sedna. Down sheer cliffs stuffed with layers of thicket, where you might toss your wish (written on a small 1" x 6" slip), down into the gaping void. Hopefully it will land on a lizard's back, sticking to its spindly little horn.

And let's say your wish makes it that far. Well, then, *down the twisted wood* goes the skinny salamander, scurrying through the decaying churches which had been **pushed** over that steep canyon ledge once and for all. And the expired priest inside, *who weathered the fall* as well, will kill the little amphibian—strangle it to death with a blessed gold chain—and save it for the annual *Getting To Know You* breakfast. He'll step on your precious little wish and, when the **thieves come**, that slip will still be there, stuck on his sole. Of course, the thieves' **preferred method of torture** is to cut a priest in thin deli-shaved slices *from top to bottom*. Who can cull evidence from that? And when they chop that last thin slice of shoe sole, they'll have that **rubber scalp** in hand for *good luck* and *good times*. But they **canoe** much too hard, these thieves. They slap their paddles swiftly in the current to get that great *outboard motor mist* going. But the shoe sole is *on a weak chain*, tied to one man's belt. And a **hairy old carp** *leaps, latches* on to that minute fraction of footwear. And the thieves *can try*, but they don't see *underwater*. If they could, they'd see that **mighty cable**, packed with millions of *needly* fiber optics. Indeed, **that fish is a peripheral plugged** right into the *core workings* of the planet Endertromb. **All it takes is one swallow** from that fish **and your wish is home free!**

And that's how wishes come true for children in this place.

Once my daughter's organ instructor had drawn up the class for the wish maker, he then followed with a class for the planet's mind reader.

```ruby
require 'endertromb'
class MindReader
  def initialize
    @minds = Endertromb::scan_for_sentience
  end
  def read
    @minds.collect do |mind|
      mind.read
    end
  end
end
```

Much as you've seen before, the **initialize** happens when a new **MindReader** object is created. This **initialize** gathers scans of the planet for mindshare. It looks like these minds are stored in an array, since they are later iterated over using the **collect** method.

Both the wish maker and the mind reader refer to a class named **Endertromb**. This class is stored in a file **endertromb.rb**, which is loaded with the code: **require 'endertromb'**. Often you'll use other classes to accomplish part of your task. Most of the latter half of this book will explore the wide variety of helpful classes that can be loaded in Ruby.

Dr. Cham Ventures Inside

But as Dr. Cham neared the castle, although the planet was aware of his thoughts, sensing his wonderment and anticipation, all Dr. Cham felt was deadness. He tromped up the steps of its open gate and through the entrance of the most beautiful architecture and was almost certain it was deserted.

For a while he knocked. Which paid off.

Blocky whale greeting.

He watched the baby whale rise like a determined balloon. He marveled at his first alien introduction and felt some concern that it had passed so quickly. Well, he would wait inside.

As he stepped through the castle door, he felt fortunate that the door hadn't been answered by a huge eagle with greedy talons, eager to play. Or a giant mouse head. Or even a man-sized hurricane. Just a tubby little choo-choo whale.

"Not a place to sit down in this castle," he said.

At first, he had thought he had just entered a very dim hallway, but as his eyes adjusted, he saw the entrance extended into a tunnel. The castle door had opened right into a passage made of long, flat slabs of rock. Some parts were congruous and resembled a corridor. Other parts narrowed, and even tilted, then finally tipped away out of view.

The passage was lit by small doorless refrigerators, big enough to hold an armful of cabbage, down by his feet. He peered inside one, which was hollow, illuminated along all sides, and turning out ice shards methodically.

He pawed the ice chips, which clung dryly to his fingertips, and he scrubbed his hands in the ice. Which left some muddy streaks on his hands, but satisfied a small part of his longing to bathe. How long had it been? Ten years? Thirty?

Along the passage, long tubes of cloth cluttered some sections. Later, bright pixel matter in porcelain scoops and buckets.

He happened upon a room which had been burrowed out of the tunnel which had a few empty turtle shells on the ground and a large illuminated wall. He stared into the room, bewildered. What could this be? In one state of mind, he thought of having a seat on a shell. This could be the entrance at last, some kind of receiving room. On the other hand, spiders could pour out of the shell's hollow when he sat. He moved on.

Meal in a Castle's Pocket

As he journeyed along the passageways (for the central tunnel forked and joined larger, vacuous caverns), he picked up themes in some locations. Groups of rooms infested with pumping machinery. Cloth and vats of glue dominated another area. He followed voices down a plush, pillowed cavity, which led him to a dead end: a curved wall with a small room carved at eye-level.

He approached the wall and, right in the cubby hole, were two aardvarks eating at a table.

They gazed at him serenely, both munching on some excavated beetle twice their size, cracked open and frozen on its back on the table.

"Hello, little puppets," he said, and they finished their bites and kept looking with their forks held aloof.

"I wish my niece Hannah were here to meet you," he told the attentive miniature aardvarks. "She'd think you were an intricate puppet show." He peered in at the dining area, shelves with sets of plates, hand towels. Half of a tiny rabbit was jutting out from the top a machine, creamy red noodles were spilling out underneath it. A door at the back of the room hung ajar. Dr. Cham could see a flickering room with chairs and whirring motors through the door.

"Any child would want this dollhouse," he said. "Hannah, my niece, as I mentioned, she has a wind-up doll that sits at a spindle and spins yarn. It's an illusion, of course. The doll produces no yarn at all."

One of the aardvarks opened a trapdoor in the floor and pressed a button down inside, which lit. Then, a small film projector slowly came up on a rod. The other aardvark sat and watched Dr. Cham.

"But Hannah still reaches down into the dollhouse and collects all the imaginary yarn into a bundle. Which she takes to her mother, my sister, who is very good at humoring Hannah. She sews a dress to the doll's dimensions, which Hannah takes back to the doll.

"And she tells the doll, 'Here, look, your hard work and perseverance has resulted in this beautiful dress. You can now accept the Chief of Police's invitation to join him tonight at the Governor's Mansion.' And she has a doll in a policeman's uniform who plays the part of the Chief. He's too scrawny to be an actual Chief, that would require quite a bit of plastic."

The aardvark responsible for the film projector loaded a reel and aimed the projector at the back wall. The film spun to life and the aardvark took a seat. A green square appeared on the wall. The attentive aardvark stared at Dr. Cham still.

"Your films are colored," said Dr. Cham. "What a lovely, little life."

The film played on: a blue square. Then, a red circle. Then, an orange square. The attentive aardvark turned away, watched the screen change to a pink triangle, and both aardvarks resumed eating.

A purple star. A red square. With quietness settling, Dr. Cham could hear notes droning from the projector. Like a slow, plodding music box trying to roll its gears along the train tracks.

"Yes, enjoy your supper," said Dr. Cham and he politely tipped his head away, marching back up the path he'd taken.

Another Dead End Where Things Began

He found himself lost in the castle's tunnels. Nothing looked familiar. He wasn't worried much, though. He was on another planet. He would be lost regardless.

He wound through the tunnels, attempting to recall his paths, but far too interested in exploring to keep track of his steps. He followed a single tunnel deep, down, down, which slanted so steeply that he had to leap across ledges and carefully watch his footholds. The gravity here seemed no different than Earth. His legs were pulled into slides just as easily.

Although he had no absolute way of knowing where he was, he felt certain that he had left the castle's boundaries. This deep, this long of a walk. It had been an hour since he'd entered through the door. And, as the tunnel wound back up, he was sure that he would emerge into a new dwelling, perhaps even a manhole which he could peek out from and see the castle. Perhaps he shouldn't have come so far down this route. He hoped nothing was hibernating down here.

The tunnel came to a stop. A dark, dead end.

At the end of the tunnels: a computer and a book.

He had time. So he read the book. He read of the foxes and their pursuit of the porcupine who stole their pickup truck. He read of the elf and the ham. He saw the pictographs of himself and found he could really relate to his own struggles. He even learned Ruby. He saw how it all ended.

Were I him, I couldn't have stomached it. But he did. And he pledged in his bosom to see things out just as they happened.

On the computer monitor, Dr. Cham saw the flashing **irb** prompt. Like Dr. Cham, you might recognize the **irb** prompt from The Tiger's Vest (the first expansion pak to this book, which includes a basic introduction to Interactive Ruby.[8])

Whereas he had just been exploring tunnels by foot, he now explored the machine's setup with the prompt. He set the book back where he had found it. He didn't need it anymore. This was all going to happen whether he used it or not.

He started with:

```
irb> Object::constants
  => ["Marshal", "String", "Dir", "LoadError", "Float", ...
and so on ]
```

This command lists all the top-level constants. Classes are also listed as constants, so this list can be great to see what's loaded into Ruby at any time.

He scanned the list for anything unfamiliar. Any classes which didn't come with Ruby. **Marshal**, **String**, **Dir**, **LoadError**, **Float**. Each of those came with Ruby.

But further down the list:

```
... "Struct", "Values", "Time", "Elevator", "Range" ...
```

Elevator? Exactly the kind of class to poke around with. He had a go.

```
irb> Elevator::methods
  => ["method", "freeze", "allocate", ... another long list
... ]
irb> Elevator::class_variables
  => ['@@diagnostic_report', '@@power_circuit_active',
'@@maintenance_password']
irb> Elevator::constants
  => []
```

8 Publisher's note: Read the archived Expansion Pak at https://poignant.guide/book/expansion-pak-1.html.

Looks like the **Elevator** class had plenty of methods. Most of these looked like they were the same methods every object has in Ruby. For example, **method**, **freeze** and **allocate** come with every class in Ruby. (**Elevator::freeze** would keep the **Elevator** class from being changed. **Elevator::allocate** would make a new **Elevator** object without calling the **initialize** method.)

The **class_variables** were interesting to Dr. Cham. This elevator appeared genuine. But no available **constants**. This tells us there are no classes nested inside the **Elevator** class.

He tried to create an **Elevator** object.

```
irb> e = Elevator::new
ArgumentError: wrong number of arguments (0 for 1), requires
a password
        from (irb):2:in `initialize'
        from (irb):2:in `new'
        from (irb):2
        from :0
```

He tried a few passwords.

```
irb> e = Elevator::new( "going up" )
AccessDeniedError: bad password
irb> e = Elevator::new( "going_up" )
AccessDeniedError: bad password
irb> e = Elevator::new( "stairs_are_bad" )
AccessDeniedError: bad password
irb> e = Elevator::new( "StairsAreBad" )
AccessDeniedError: bad password
```

That was useless. *Oh, wait!* The maintenance password. Listed in the **class_variables**.

```
irb> Elevator::maintenance_password
NoMethodError: undefined method `maintenance_password' for
Elevator:Class
        from (irb):1
        from :0
```

Hmm. Instance variables are only available inside an object. And class variables are only available inside a class. How to get at that password?

```
irb> class Elevator
irb>    def Elevator.maintenance_password
irb>      @@maintenance_password
irb>    end
irb> end
  => nil
irb> Elevator::maintenance_password
  => "stairs_are_history!"
```

Alright! He got the password. Did you see that?

He added a class method to the **Elevator** class. Isn't that great how you can start a new class definition for **Elevator** and Ruby just adds your changes to the existing class definition?

Class methods are usually called with the **double colon**. But, a period is fine as well. Since **Elevator** is a class itself, Ruby will figure that if you call **Elevator.maintenance_password**, you're calling a class method. The double colon simply helps make class methods obvious to the reader.

And justly so. Class methods are a bit unusual. Normally you won't want to store information directly inside of a class. However, if you have a bit of information that you need to share among all objects of a class, then you have a good reason to use the class for storage. It's understandable that the **@@maintenance_password** would be stored in the class, instead of in each separate object. This way, the objects can simply reach up into the class and see the shared password.

Here's probably how the password protection works.

```
class Elevator
  def initialize( pass )
    raise AccessDeniedError, "bad password" \
      unless pass.equals? @@maintenance_password
  end
end
```

Passwording a class like this is pointless, since anything in Ruby can be altered and overwritten and remolded. Dr. Cham had the password and ownership of the elevator is his.

```
irb> e = Elevator.new( "stairs_are_history!" )
  => #<Elevator:0x81f12f4 @level=4>
irb> e.level = 1
```

Dr. Cham was standing right there when the elevator doors, off behind the computer terminal, opened for him. With an exasperated sense of accomplishment and a good deal of excitement surrounding all of the events that lie ahead, he stepped into the elevator and pressed 4.

3. The Continued Story of My Daughter's Organ Instructor

I know you may be alarmed to hear that I have a daughter. You think my writing is indicative of a palsied or infantile mind. Well, please rest. I don't have a daughter. But I can't let that stop me from sorting out her musical training.

As I was related these elaborate histories of the planet Endertromb, I found myself wandering through hallways, running my fingertips along the tightly buttoned sofas and soaking myself in the saturated bellowings of the pipes, as played by my daughter's organ instructor. His notes resounded so deep and hollow in the walls of his manor that I began to casually mistake them for an ominous silence, and found it even easier to retreat into deep space with my thoughts. To think upon the ancient planet and its darker philosophies: its flesh temples, tanned from the dermal remains of its martyrs; its whale cartels, ingesting their enemies and holding them within for decades, dragging them up and down the staircases of ribs; its poison fogs and its painful doorways; and, the atrocious dynasties of The Originals, the species which claims fathership to all of the intelligent beings across the universe.

But, eventually, I'd hear those pipes of a higher octave sing and I'd be back in the very same breezy afternoon where I'd left.

An Evening of Unobstructed Voltage

I dug up this article from **The Consistent Reminder**, a Connecticut newspaper which ran the four star review of Dr. Cham. Midgie Dare, the book reviewer who suddenly opened her critical eye to anything tangible, praised the Doctor for his manners and innovations in the very same daily edition that she defamed cantaloupe and docked Manitoba for having crackly telephone service.
  I got a kick out of the end of her article. Here you go.

He dismounted his horse with unquestionable care for anyone who might be in the vicinity. Attentive of all sides, he lowered himself from the saddle gently, slowing to a pace which must be measured in micrometers per second to be appreciated. Those of us in his company found ourselves with maws agape, watching his boot touch down upon the ground. So precise and clean a step that it seemed it would never meet the earth, only hover slight above it. Then, before the landing had actually registered with any of us, we were off to the cuisine, whisked away in the shroud of gaiety that was always right in front of Harold Cham, always just behind him, and most especially concentrate directly in his own luminary self. He also carried loosely at his side a capitally ignorant statesman's daughter, who spared us no leave from her constant criticisms of atheists and railway routes. "At home, my efforts to light a candle were trounced upon by further train rumblings, which thrusted the match in my hand nearer the curtains!" She derided Dr. Cham for his waning grip on her forearm and became jealous when he was able to tune into a pleasurable woman's voice on the radio once we returned to the residence. The dusk did settle, however, and we found ourselves in a communal daze beneath the thick particles of cotton drift that wafted through the polished piano room, quite entertained by the **Afternoon Nap Program**, which played their phonograph so quietly at the station that we could only hear the scratching of dead Napoleon's sleeves across the bedsheets. I felt a great shriek inside me at the thought! Still, on yonder chairs, the two lovers kept an abrupt distance between themselves and I felt encompassed by Dr. Cham's warm gaze and his playful tip of the sherry glass.

How interesting that even the breeze of our planet is quite a strange thing to some outsiders. For he had also told me of the travelers from Rath-d, who ventured to Earth five centuries ago, but quickly dissipated in our air currents since they and their crafts and their armor were all composed of charcoal.

I had sat at the organ, listening to his faint tales of his colony, while he punctuated his symphonies to greater volumes and the story would disappear for awhile, until the coda came back around. He spoke of he and his brothers piling into the hollow of his mother's tail and tearing the waxy crescent tissue from the inner wall. Juicy and spongy and syrupy soap which bleached their mouths and purged their esophagus as it went down. They chewed and chomped the stuff and it foamed. After they ate, they blew bubbles at each other, each bubble filled with a dense foam, which they slept upon. And early in the morning, when mother opened her tail again, she watched serenely as her babies lay cradled in the stew of dark meatballs and sweet, sticky froth.

He spelled out all the tastes of Endertromb. Of their salmon's starchy organs, which cooked into a pasta, and its eyes which melted into rich cream. Of their buttermelon with tentacles. And he was just beginning to appreciate the delicacies as a child, only to be lifted from a schoolyard by a pair of upright pygmy elephants who reached at him, through the heavens, and snatched upon his collar with a vast length of crane.

They transplanted him on Earth, led him from their craft, trumpeting their snouts loudly for the city of Grand Rapids to hear, then left, weeping and embracing each other.

"But, strangely (em-pithy-dah), I learned upon, played upon (pon-shoo) the organs on my home (oth-rea) planet," he said.

My daughter's organ instructor speaks these extra words you see in parentheses. Who knows if they are from his native tongue or if they are his own soundful hiccups. He keeps another relic from Endertromb as well: he has twelve names.

"No, (wen-is-wen)," he said. "I have one name (im-apalla) which is said (iff) many-many different ways."

I call him Paij-ree in the morning and Paij-plo in the later evening. Since it is day as I write, I will call him Paij-ree here.

Mumble-Free Earplugs

So I told Paij-ree, "Paij-ree, I am writing a book. To teach the world Ruby."

"Oh, (pill-nog-pill-yacht) nice," he said. He's known Ruby longer than I have, but still: *I* will be my daughter's Ruby instructor.

And I said, "Paij-ree, you are in the book. And the stories of your planet." I talk to him like he's E.T. I don't know why. Just like how I said next, "And then maybe someday you can go home to your mom and dad!"

To which he said, "(pon-shoo) (pon-shoo) (em-pithy-dah)." Which is his way of speaking out loud his silence and awe.

He wanted to see what I'd written, so I showed him this short method I've written for you.

```ruby
def wipe_mutterings_from( sentence )
  while sentence.include? '('
    open = sentence.index( '(' )
    close = sentence.index( ')', open )
    sentence[open..close] = '' if close
  end
end
```

"Can you see what this does, Paij-ree? Any old Smotchkkiss can use this method to take all the incoherent babblings out of your speaking," I said.

And I fed something he said earlier into the method.

```ruby
what_he_said = "But, strangely (em-pithy-dah),
  I learned upon, played upon (pon-shoo) the
  organs on my home (oth-rea) planet."
wipe_mutterings_from( what_he_said )
print what_he_said
```

And it came out as a rather plain sentence.

```
But, strangely ,
I learned upon, played upon the
organs on my home planet.
```

"You shouldn't use that (wary-to) while loop," he said. "There are lovelier, (thopt-er), gentler ways."

In the **wipe_mutterings_from** method, I'm basically searching for opening parentheses. When I find one, I scan for a closing paren which follows it. Once I've found both, I replace them and their contents with an empty string. The **while** loop continues until all parentheses are gone. The mutterings are removed and the method ends.

"Now that I look at this method," I said. "I see that there are some confusing aspects and some ways I could do this better." Please don't look down on me as your teacher for writing some of this code. I figure that it's okay to show you some sloppy techniques to help you work through them with me. So let's.

Okay, **Confusing Aspect No. 1**: This method cleans a string. But what if we accidentally give it a **File**? Or a number? What happens? What if we run **wipe_mutterings_from(1)**?

If we give **wipe_mutterings_from** the number 1, Ruby will print the following and exit.

```
NoMethodError: undefined method `include?' for 1:Fixnum
        from (irb):2:in `wipe_mutterings_from'
        from (irb):8
```

What you see here is a rather twisted and verbose (but at times very helpful) little fellow called the **backtrace**. He's a wound-up policeman who, at the slightest sign of trouble, immediately apprehends any and all suspects, pinning them against the wall and spelling out their rights so quickly that none can quite hear it all. But it's plain that there's a problem. And, of course, it's all a big misunderstanding, right?

When Ruby reads you these Miranda rights, listen hardest to the beginning. The first line is often all you need. In this first line is contained the essential message. And in the above, the first line is telling us that there is no **include?** method for the number 1. Remember, when we were talking about the **reverse** method in the last chapter? Back then, I said, "**a lot of methods are only available with certain types of values.**" Both **reverse** and **include?** are methods which work with strings but are meaningless and unavailable for numbers.

To be clear: the method tries to use to the number. The method will start with **sentence** set to 1. Then, it hits the second line: **while sentence.include? '('**. Numbers have no **include?** method. Great, the backtrace has shown us where the problem is. I didn't expect anyone to pass in a number, so I'm using methods that don't work with numbers.

See, this is just it. Our method is its own little pocket tool, right? It acts as its own widget independent of anything else. To anyone out there using the **wipe_mutterings_from** method, should they pass in a number, they'll be tossed this panic message that doesn't make sense to them. They'll be asked to poke around inside the method, which really isn't their business. They don't know their way around in there.

Fortunately, we can throw our own errors, our own **exceptions**, which may make more sense to someone who inadvertently hands the wrong object in for cleaning.

```
def wipe_mutterings_from( sentence )
  unless sentence.respond_to? :include?
    raise ArgumentError,
      "cannot wipe mutterings from a #{ sentence.class }"
  end
  while sentence.include? '('
    open = sentence.index( '(' )
    close = sentence.index( ')', open )
    sentence[open..close] = '' if close
  end
end
```

This time, if we pass in a number (again, the number 1), we'll get something more sensible.

```
ArgumentError: cannot wipe mutterings from a Fixnum
        from (irb):3:in `wipe_mutterings_from'
        from (irb):12
```

The **respond_to?** method is really nice and I plead that you never forget it's there. The **respond_to?** checks any object to be sure that it has a certain method. It then gives back a **true** or **false**. In the above case, the incoming **sentence** object is checked for an **include?** method. If no **include?** method is found, then we raise the error.

You might be wondering why I used a symbol with **respond_to?**. I used a symbol **:include?** instead of a string **'include?'**. Actually, either will work with **respond_to?**.

Usually symbols are used when you are passing around the name of a method or any other Ruby construct. It's more efficient, but it also catches the eye. The **respond_to?** asks Ruby to look inside itself and see if a method is available. We're talking to Ruby, so the symbol helps denote that. It's not a big deal, Ruby just recognizes symbols quicker than strings.

Now, **Confusing Aspect No. 2**: Have you noticed how our method changes the sentence?

```
something_said = "A (gith) spaceship."
wipe_mutterings_from( something_said )
print something_said
```

Did you notice this? In the first line of the above code, the **something_said** variable contains the string **"A (gith) spaceship."**. But, after the method invocation, on the third line, we print the **something_said** variable and by then it contains the cleaned string **"A spaceship."**.

How does this work? How does the method change the string? Shouldn't it make a copy of the string before changing it?

Yes, absolutely, it should! **It's bad manners to change strings like that.** We've used **gsub** and **gsub!** in the last chapter. Do you remember which of those two methods is a **destructive method**, which changes strings directly?

Either we need to call this method **wipe_mutterings_from!** (as a courtesy to all the other good folks out there that might use this method) or change the method to work on a copy of the string rather than the real thing. Which is an easy change! We just need to **dup** the string.

```ruby
def wipe_mutterings_from( sentence )
  unless sentence.respond_to? :include?
    raise ArgumentError,
      "cannot wipe mutterings from a #{ sentence.class }"
  end
  sentence = sentence.dup
  while sentence.include? '('
    open = sentence.index( '(' )
    close = sentence.index( ')', open )
    sentence[open..close] = '' if close
  end
  sentence
end
```

The **dup** method makes a copy of any object. Look at that line we added again on its own:

```ruby
sentence = sentence.dup
```

What a peculiar line of code. How does **sentence** become a copy of **sentence**? Does it erase itself? What happens to the original **sentence**? Does it disappear?

Remember that variables are just nicknames. When you see **sentence = "A (gith) spaceship."**, you see Ruby creating a string and then giving that string a nickname.

Likewise, when you see **sentence = sentence.dup**, you see Ruby creating a new string and then giving that string a nickname. This is handy inside your method because now **sentence** is a nickname for a new copy of the string that you can safely use **without changing the string that was passed into the method**.

You'll see plenty of examples of variable names being reused.

```ruby
x = 5
x = x + 1
# x now equals 6

y = "Endertromb"
y = y.length
# y now equals 10
```

```
z = :include?
z = "a string".respond_to? z
# z now equals true
```

And, yes, sometimes objects disappear. **If you can't get to an object through a variable, then Ruby will figure you are done with it and will get rid of it.** Periodically, Ruby sends out its **garbage collector** to set these objects free. Every object is kept in your computer's memory until the garbage collector gets rid of it.

Oh, and one more thing about **dup**. Some things can't be dup'd. Numbers, for instance. Symbols (which look like **:death**) are identical when spelled the same. Like numbers.

Also, some of the special variables: **nil**, **true**, **false**. These are things that Ruby won't let you alter, so there's so point making a copy anyway. I mean, imagine if you could change **false** to be **true**. The whole thing becomes a lie.

An Excerpt from The Scarf Eaters
(from Chapter VII: When Push Comes to Shove—or Love.)
"Never say my name again!" screamed Chester, and with the same gusto, he turned back to the **File > Publish Settings...** *dialog to further optimize his movie down to a measly 15k.*

Perhaps **Confusing Aspect No. 3** is a simple one. I'm using those square brackets on the string. I'm treating the string like it's an Array or Hash. I can do that. Because strings have a **[]** method.

When used on a string, the square brackets will extract part of the string. Again, slots for a forklift's prongs. The string is a long shelf and the forklift is pulling out a slab of the string.

Inside the brackets, we pass the *index*. It's the label we've placed right between the prongs where the worker can see it. When it comes to strings, we can use a variety of objects as our index.

```ruby
str = "A string is a long shelf of letters and spaces."
puts str[0]          # prints 'A'
puts str[0..-1]      # prints 'A string is a long shelf of letters
and spaces.'
puts str[1..-2]      # prints ' string is a long shelf of letters
and spaces'
puts str[0, 3]       # prints 'A s'
puts str['shelf']    # prints 'shelf'
```

Alright, the last **Confusing Aspect No. 4**: this method can be sent into an endless loop. You can give this method a string which will cause the method to hang and never come back. Take a look at the method. Can you throw in a muddy stick to clog the loop?

```ruby
def wipe_mutterings_from( sentence )
  unless sentence.respond_to? :include?
    raise ArgumentError,
      "cannot wipe mutterings from a #{ sentence.class }"
  end
  sentence = sentence.dup
  while sentence.include? '('
    open = sentence.index( '(' )
    close = sentence.index( ')', open )
    sentence[open..close] = '' if close
  end
  sentence
end
```

Here, give the muddy stick a curve before you jam it.

```ruby
muddy_stick = "Here's a ( curve."
wipe_mutterings_from( muddy_stick )
```

Why does the method hang? Well, the **while** loop waits until all the open parentheses are gone before it stops looping. And it only replaces open parentheses that have a matching closing parentheses. So, if no closing paren is found, the open paren won't be replaced and the **while** will never be satisfied.

How would you rewrite this method? Me, I know my way around Ruby, so I'd use a regular expression.

```
def wipe_mutterings_from( sentence )
  unless sentence.respond_to? :gsub
    raise ArgumentError,
      "cannot wipe mutterings from a #{ sentence.class }"
  end
  sentence.gsub( /\(([-\w]+\)/, '' )
end
```

Do your best to think through your loops. It's especially easy for **while** and **until** loops to get out of hand. Best to use an iterator. And we'll get to regular expressions in time.

In summary, here's what we've learned about writing methods:

1. Don't be surprised if people pass unexpected objects into your methods. If you absolutely can't use what they give you, **raise** an error.

2. It's poor etiquette to change objects your method is given. Use **dup** to make a copy. Or find a method like **gsub** that automatically makes a copy as it does its job.

3. The square brackets can be used to lookup parts inside any **Array**, **Hash** or **String** objects, as these objects provide a **[]** method. Also, since these objects provide a **[]=** method, the square brackets can be used in assignment (on the left-hand side of the equals sign) to change the parts of those objects.

4. Watch for runaway loops. Avoid **while** and **until** if you can.

The Mechanisms of Name-Calling

Forthwith there is a rustling in the trees behind Paij-ree's house and it turns out to be a man falling from the sky. His name is Doug and he sells cats.

So, just as he comes into to view, when his shadow (and the shadows of the cats tied to his foot) obscures the bird on the lawn that we're trying to hit with a racquetball, as he's squeezing a wisp of helium from his big balloon, we shout, "Hello, Doug!"

And he says, "Hello, Gonk-ree! Hello, Why!"

Paij-ree checks his pockets to be sure he has the dollar-twenty-seven he'll need in order to buy the three cats he'll need to keep the furnace stoked and the satellite dish turning. These cats generate gobs of static once Paij-ree tosses them in the generator, where they'll be outnumbered by the giant glass rods, which caress the cats continually—But, wait! Did you see how the cat broker called him Gonk-ree?

And he calls him Gonk-ree in the morning and Gonk-plo at night.

So the suffix is definitely subject to the sunlight. As far as I can tell, the prefix indicates the namecaller's relationship to Paij-ree.

```ruby
class String

  # The parts of my daughter's organ
  # instructor's name.
  @@syllables = [
    { 'Paij' => 'Personal',
      'Gonk' => 'Business',
      'Wert' => 'Father',
      'Onnn' => 'Mother' },
    { 'ree' => 'AM',
      'plo' => 'PM' }
  ]

  # A method to determine what a
  # certain name of his means.
  def name_significance
    parts = self.split( '-' )
    syllables = @@syllables.dup
    signif = parts.collect do |p|
      syllables.shift[p]
    end
    signif.join( ' ' )
  end

end
```

Now I've gone beyond just showing you sloppy code. Here be a grave debauchery and a crime against nature. A crime most languages won't allow you to commit. We're changing the **String, one of the core classes of Ruby**!

"I know this is a bit dangerous," I said, when I passed this one under Paij-ree's nose. "I hope nobody gets hurt."

"Every Smotchkkiss must taste what this (kep-yo-iko) danger does," he said. "Dogs and logs and swampy bogs (kul-ip), all must be tasted." And he took a swig of his Beagle Berry marsh drink.

So what is it that I'm adding to the **String** class? Two things: a class variable and a method. A normal **instance method**.

I like to look at the **at** symbol as a character meaning **attribute**. The **double at** stands for **attribute all**. A class variable. All instances of a class can look at this variable and it is the same for all of them. The **@@syllables** variable is an Array that can now be used inside the String class.

The new method is **name_significance** and this new method can be used with any string.

```
print "Paij-ree".name_significance
#=> Personal AM
```

As you can see, Paij-ree is a personal name. A name friends use in the early hours.

Make sure you see the line of code which uses **self**. This is a special variable, a variable which represents the object whose method you are calling. To simplify things a bit, let's try making a method which breaks up a string on its dashes.

```
class String
  def dash_split
    self.split( '-' )
  end
end
```

Again, here's a method which can be used with any string.

```
"Gonk-plo".dash_split
#=> ['Gonk', 'plo']
```

Using **self** marks the beginning of crossing over into many of the more advanced ideas in Ruby. This is definition language. You're defining a method, designing it before it gets used. You're preparing for the existence of an object which uses that method. You're saying, "When **dash_split** gets used, there will be a string at that time which is the one we're dash-splitting. And **self** is a special variable which refers to that string."

Ruby is a knockout definition language. A succulent and brain-splitting discussion is coming your way deeper in this book.

Most often you won't need to use **self** explicitly, since you can call methods directly from inside other method definitions.

```
class String
  def dash_split; split( '-' ); end
end
```

In the **name_significance** method, find the loop. Learning about **Array#collect** is essential. Let's look close.

```
signif = parts.collect do |p|
  syllables.shift[p]
end
```

The **parts** Array contains the separated name. **['Paij', 'plo']**, for instance. We're iterating through each item in that Array with **collect**. But **collect** steps beyond what **each** does. Like **each**, collect slides each item down the chute as a block variable. And then, at the end of the block, **collect keeps the answer the block gives back and adds it to a new Array**. The **collect** method is the perfect way of building a new Array which is based on the items in an existing Array.

Doug has three cats for sale. One is twelve cents, one is sixty-three cents, one is nine cents. Let's see how much each cat would cost if we added a 20% tip.

```
catsandtips = [0.12, 0.63, 0.09].collect { |catcost|
  catcost + ( catcost * 0.20 ) }
```

I say Paij-ree's property is a very charming section of woods when it's not raining cats and Doug. For many days, Paij-ree and I camped in tents by the river behind his house, subsisting on smoked blackbird and whittling little sleeping Indians by the dusklight. On occasion he would lose a game of spades and I knew his mind was distracted, thinking of Endertromb. All of this must have been stirring inside of him for sometime. I was the first ear he'd ever had.

"I just came from Ambrose," I said. "Sort of my own underground home, a place where elves strive to perfect animals."

He mumbled and nodded. "You can't be (poth-in-oin) part of (in) such things."

"You think we will fail?"

"I (preep) have been there before," he said. And then, he spoke of the Lotteries.

4. The Goat Wants to Watch a Whole Film

Blinky, winky, a goat... awakes...

The elevator had opened into a green room full of shelves and file cabinets. Reels of tape and film canisters and video tape everywhere. Dr. Cham hadn't a clue what most of it was. All he saw was a big, futuristic mess.

He called out again, stumbling through alleys of narrow shelves, "Hello-o-o?? I'm looking for intelligent life! I'm a space traveler!" He tripped when his foot slid right into a VCR slot. "Any other beings I can communicate with?"

Hand cupped around mouth, he yelled, "Hello-o-o?"

"Crying out loud." The sleepy goat came tromping down the aisle.

The goat already knows Dr. Cham.

"I hate that book," said the goat. "I believe the author is disingenuous."

"Really?" asked Dr. Cham.

"I'm sure it's all true. It's just so heavily embellished. I'm like: Enough already. I get it. Cut it out."

"I'm not quite sure what to make of it," said the Doctor. "It seems like an honest effort. I actually wrote something in Ruby back there."

"It doesn't give goats a very good name," said the goat.

"But you are the only goat in the book," said the Doctor.

"And I'm totally misquoted."

The mechanics behind devouring Dr. Cham.

The goat closed his mouth and Dr. Cham held his heart.

"I'm actually very literate," said the goat. "Albeit, more recently, I've switched to movies. I love foreign films. One of my relatives just brought back *Ishtar* from your planet. Wow, that was excellent."

"I haven't been to my planet in a long time. It would be difficult to consider it my home at this stage."

"Well, Warren Beatty is delightful. His character is basically socially crippled. He actually tries to kill himself, but Dustin Hoffman sits in the window sill and starts crying and singing this totally hilarious heartbreak song. I've got it here, you should see it."

"Can I get something to eat?" asked the Doctor. And he still felt filthy.

"How about we watch a film and you can have a buttermelon with tentacles?" said the goat.

So, they worked their way back toward the goat's projector. Back by the freezer locker, they sat on a giant rug and broke off the appendages of frozen buttermelons. The shell was solid, but once it cracked, rich fruit cream was in abundance. Sweet to taste and a very pleasant scent.

"First film, you've got to see," said the goat. "Locally filmed and produced. I'm good friends with the lady who did casting. Dated her for awhile. Knew everyone who was going to play the different roles long before it was announced."

The goat set the projector by Dr. Cham. "I've got the music on the surround sound. You can man the knob."

TURNING THE KNOB ON THE FILMSTRIP, DR. CHAM BEGAN WATCHING ALONG WITH THE GOAT, AS THE SOUND- TRACK ECHOED NOISY LAVA & WIND & TRUMPETS.

THE FILMSTRIP STARTS WITH THESE ANIMALS CALLED **THE ORIGINALS,** WHO CLAIMED TO BE THE 1ST CREATURES TO EVER LIVE.

IN FACT, THEY CLAIMED THEY WERE THE 1st OF ANYTHING EVER TO EXIST ANYWHERE.

SIMPLY BECAUSE THEY HAD NO PROOF OF ANY- THING ELSE. ALL AROUND THEIR PLANET WAS BLACK DARKNESS AND MAYBE ONE STAR REALLY FAR AWAY THAT GAVE A FEW SLIVERS OF LIGHT.

YES, THEY WERE PRIMITIVE, BUT THEY MANAGED TO INVENT A FEW HEAT LAMPS & RAISE THE 1st AVOCADOES EVER.

BUT THEY DID NOT HAVE ANY BUCKETS YET, SO THEY HAD TO CARRY THE RIVER WATER IN THEIR MOUTHS ALL THE WAY BACK TO THEIR PLANTS.

AND THEY LACKED INTEL- LEGENCE AND ANY KIND OF DIS- CIPLINE, SO THEY NEVER REALLY WENT TO COLLEGE OR AMOUNTED TO ANYTHING.

MAYBE THEY WERE WORTH- LESS. MAYBE THEY SHOULDN'T HAVE BEEN ALLOWED TO STAY ALIVE. I THINK THEY WERE JUST VERY SIMPLE.

AS TIME PASSED, THE BLACK DARK- NESS FADED AND THEY SAW OTHER PLANETS.

AND NEW ANI- MALS CAME TO THEIR PLANET ON SPACEBOATS AND VERY LONG LADDERS.

THESE NEW ANI- MALS BUILT THEIR OWN CITIES AND WANTED EVERYONE TO VOTE FOR THEM.

BUT **THE ORI- GINALS** DIDN'T HUMOR THESE ALIENS WHAT- SOEVER. AND I AM SAD TO SAY THAT THEY TOOK TO MEAN-SPIRITED BERATING.

The Originals and their lonesome planet.

```
we want a tambourine!
            /
          |   we want all a tambourine!
          |        /
          \__   |
         /   o o \__/\__/\_
       /.         \ o o \____
      /'       ----/            \
_____ /    '    / /.\\    ⫯------/
     /        /         /      \\
    /        /        ///
   /so               \
         /\    \me time\\..
      /pp/   \s these pictur\\
      /es/    \don't w\ \ork out\
    ***        *** right but i
      think this time
          they did
            ooo o
             oo
            o
         o
       {o}
     ^
```

Dr. Cham's mind wandered at this point in the presentation, just as the land war mounted between the two throngs of animal settlers. The details of their wars and campaigns continued to consume the spool of transparent film that Dr. Cham was feeding through the projector.

War after war after war. The Sieging of Elmer Lake. The Last Stand of Newton P. Giraffe and Sons. Dog Invasion of Little Abandoned Cloud. No animals died in these wars. Most often an attack consisted of bopping another animal on the head. And they philipped each other's noses. But, believe me, it was humiliating.

Blasted crying shame. Things could have worked out.

The Birth of an Object

"Don't worry," said the goat, anxious to sway Dr. Cham's attention back to the film. "Things *do* work out."

In Ruby, the Object is the very center of all things. It is The Original.

```
class ToastyBear < Object; end
```

The angle bracket indicates **inheritance**. This means that the new **ToastyBear** class is a new class based on the **Object** class. Every method that **Object** has will be available in **ToastyBear**. Constants available in **Object** will be available in **ToastyBear**.

But every object inherits from **Object**. The code...

```
class ToastyBear; end
```

Is identical to...

```
class ToastyBear < Object; end
```

Inheritance is handy. You can create species of objects which relate to each other. Often, when you're dissecting a problem, you'll come across various objects which share attributes. You can save yourself work by inheriting from classes which already solve part of that problem.

You may have a **UnitedStatesAddress** class which stores the address, city, state, and zip code for someone living in the United States. When you start storing addresses from England, you could add a **UnitedKingdomAddress** class. If you then ensure that both addresses inherit from a parent **Address** class, you can design your mailing software to accept any kind of address.

```
def mail_them_a_kit( address )
  unless address.is_a? Address
    raise ArgumentError, "No Address object found."
  end
  print address.formatted
end
```

Also, inheritance is great if you want to override certain behaviors in a class. For example, perhaps you want to make your own slight variation to the **Array** class. You want to enhance the **join** method. But if you change **Array#join** directly, you will affect other classes in Ruby that use Arrays.

So you start your own class called **ArrayMine**, which is based on The Original **Array**.

```ruby
class ArrayMine < Array
  # Build a string from this array, formatting each
  # entry then joining them together.
  def join( sep = $,, format = "%s" )
    collect do |item|
      sprintf( format, item )
    end.join( sep )
  end
end
```

ArrayMine is now a custom **Array** class with its own **join** method. **Array** is the **superclass** of **ArrayMine**. Every class has a **superclass** method where you can verify this relationship.

```
irb> ArrayMine.superclass
  => Array
```

Perfect. We manage a hotel and we have an **Array** of our room sizes: **[3, 4, 6]**. Let's get it nicely printed for a brochure.

```ruby
rooms = ArrayMine[3, 4, 6]
print "We have " + rooms.join( ", ", "%d bed" ) +
" rooms available."
```

Which prints, "We have 3 bed, 4 bed, 6 bed rooms available."

Dr. Cham was looking around for a bathroom, but archival video tape was everywhere. He eventually found a place, it may have been a bathroom. It had a metal bin. More importantly, it was dark and out of eyesight.

While he's in there, let me add that while The Originals slaughtered The Invaders to prove their rights as First Creatures, the Ruby Object doesn't have any such dispute. It is the absolute king Object the First.

Watch.

```
irb> Class.superclass
  => Module
irb> Kernel.class
  => Module
irb> Module.superclass
  => Object
irb> Object.superclass
  => nil
```

Even **Class** is an **Object**! See, although classes are the definition language for objects, we still call class methods on them and treat them like objects occasionally. It may seem like a dizzying circle, but it's truly a very strict parentage. And it ensures that when you alter the **Object**, you alter **everything in Ruby**. Which is impossibly scary and all-powerful and cataclysmic and awesome! **Ruby does not restrict you, my sister, my brother!**

Between **Class** and **Object**, do you see **Module**? If **Object** is the king, the one who has sired every other part of Ruby, then **Module** is the poor waifish nun, shielding and protecting all her little Ruby townspeople children. (To complete the analogy: **Class** is the village school teacher and **Kernel** is the self-important colonel.)

The whole point of **Module**'s existence is to give food and shelter to code. Methods can stay dry under **Module**'s shawl. **Module** can hold classes and constants and variables of any kind.

"But what does a Module *do*?" you ask. "How is it gainfully employed??"

"That's all it does!!" I retort, stretching out my open palms in the greatest expression of futility known to man. "Now hear me—for I will never speak it again—that Module Mother Superior has given these wretched objects a place to stay!!"

```
# See, here is the module -- where else could our code
possibly stay?
module WatchfulSaintAgnes

  # A CONSTANT is laying here by the doorway.  Fine.
  TOOTHLESS_MAN_WITH_FORK = ['man', 'fork', 'exposed
gums']

  # A Class is eating, living well in the kitchen.
  class FatWaxyChild; end

  # A Method is hiding back in the banana closet, God
knows why.
  def timid_foxfaced_girl; {'please' => 'i want an acorn
please'}; end

end
```

Now you have to go through Saint Agnes to find them.

```
>> WatchfulSaintAgnes::TOOTHLESS_MAN_WITH_FORK
=> ["man", "fork", "exposed gums"]
>> WatchfulSaintAgnes::FatWaxyChild.new
=> #<WatchfulSaintAgnes::FatWaxyChild:0xb7d2ad78>
>> WatchfulSaintAgnes::instance_methods
=> ["timid_foxfaced_girl"]
```

Always remember that a **Module** is only an inn. A roof over their heads. It is not a self-aware **Class** and, therefore, cannot be brought to life with **new**.

```
>> WatchfulSaintAgnes.new
NoMethodError: undefined method `new' for
WatchfulSaintAgnes:Module
        from (irb):2
```

St. Agnes has given up her whole life in order that she may care for these desperate bits of code. Please. Don't take that away from her.

If you wanted to steal from St. Agnes, though, I can help you. You can bring in a larger abbey to swallow up the ministry of **WatchfulSaintAgnes** and then what is she left with?

For this you can use **extend**, which will pull all the methods from a module into a class or an object.

```
>> class TheTimeWarnerAolCitibankCaringAndLovingFacility; end
>> TheTimeWarnerAolCitibankCaringAndLovingFacility.extend
WatchfulSaintAgnes
>> TheTimeWarnerAolCitibankCaringAndLovingFacility::instance_methods
=> ["timid_foxfaced_girl"]
```

In truth, no one's *stolen* from **WatchfulSaintAgnes**, only borrowed. The **timid_foxfaced_girl** now has two addresses.

You gotta admit. The old abbey can get bought out a zillion times and that little fox-faced girl will *still* be back in the banana closet wanting an acorn! Too bad we can't feed her. She's a method with no arguments.

When Dr. Cham came out refreshed, the filmstrip was a bit behind. But the goat hadn't noticed, so the Doctor advanced frames until it made some sense.

The goats that told a planet it was ugly.

SO THE CREATURES WERE ALL AT WAR, MUCH LIKE THE HEALTH BOOKS DESCRIBE THE WAR BETWEEN FATTY TISSUES + AMINO ACIDS WHICH WAGES CONTINUALLY INSIDE YOUR BODY...

WHICH MEANT THEY OFTEN FOUGHT OVER STUPID THINGS LIKE **KORMO**, WHICH WAS BASICALLY A VERY POPULAR BRAND OF TUNA SAND-WICHES.

AND THE PRICE OF LEMON KITS WAS HIGH.

HOWEVER, TWO GOATS SHOWED UP, ASKING WHICH SIDE THEY WERE ON. NEITHER COULD REMEMBER.

THe ORIGINALS THOUGHT THAT PROBABLY THE GOATS WERE WITH THEM. GOATS HAD BEEN AROUND, RIGHT? BUT...

THE INVADERS SWORE THEY HAD BROUGHT GOATS!!

"YOU'RE LATE!" THEY SAID.

BUT HERE'S THE DEAL: ONE GOAT WAS AN ORIGINAL AND THE OTHER WAS NOT AND THEY WERE BLUFFING. AND IN LOVE. AND LYING.

(YES, THESE WERE THE PARENTS OF THE

ABSOLUTELY ENGROSSED GOAT FRIEND OF DR. CHAM.)

"WELL, MAYBE," THE GOATS SAID, "MAYBE WE'RE ON THE WRONG PLANET. THIS PLANET LOOKS TOO OLD."

IT'S THE OLDEST PLANET!

IS IT SURELY?

AND EVEN THOUGH THE INVADERS DIDN'T REALLY BELIEVE THAT **THe ORIGINALS** WERE THE 1ST ANIMALS EVER... AND THAT THEIR PLANET WAS THE OLDEST...

THEY STARTED TO SEE HOW DECREPIT IT REALLY WAS.

So the invaders left the planet.

"This planet *is* decrepit," said Dr. Cham. "The castle is nice. But inside it's a disaster."

"The whole castle look is a projection," said the goat. "All the flowers and apple blossoms and the sky even. It's a low-resolution projection."

"Yes? It is enchanting."

"I guess."

ALL THE ANIMALS HAPPENED UPON A PLANET CALLED **PEOPLEMUD** (AND DR. CHAM RECOGNIZED THIS PLANET FROM HIS TRAVEL — IT WAS THE VERY ONE HE'D LEFT BEHIND.)

SO THEY FLEW DOWN TO INHABIT IT... BUT BLOOD AT ONCE POURED FROM THE ANIMALS' MOUTHS...

BLLUOOSHKMRO GOOD GRAVES! ...AND A GREAT EGG YOLK SPILLED OVER THE PICTURE...

The spool ends.

"That's messed up!" said the goat. "That's not the way the film ends! There's no blood! What happened? What happened? Did you screw up the knob, idiot?"

"Well, I don't know," said Dr. Cham. He turned the knob reverse and forward. Tapped the lens.

"Check the film! Check the film!"

Dr. Cham pulled out a length of film from the projection feed, melted and dripping from its end.

"Curse that! These projectors are quality! I've never had this happen. There's no way."

Hunting For a Voice

"I don't think it was the projector," said Dr. Cham. "Something flew across that screen and uttered a blistering moan."

"I don't have any dupes of that movie," said the goat somberly. "And that girl. That casting director. I never see her anymore."

Dr. Cham stood up and looked over the dumpy aisles of magnetic carnage, searching.

"Oh, hey, you should call that girl," the goat went on. "You could talk to her, get an understanding. Tell her about me. Don't act like your my friend, just, you know, 'Oh, that guy? Yeah, whatta maroon.'"

Dr. Cham spotted the doorway and exited.

The hallways were an entirely new world of mess. In the goat's archives, the shelves had been messy. In the hallway, shelves were completely tipped. Sinks were falling through the ceiling. The Doctor ventured under the debris, kicking through plywood when necessary.

"You shouldn't be out here," said the goat. "You're on someone else's property at this point. A couple of pygmy elephants own all this. They're nasty guys. They'll beat the crap outta you with their trunks. They ball it up and just whack ya."

Dr. Cham pushed a file cabinet out of his way, which fell through a flimsy wall, then through the floor of the next room over. And they heard it fall through several floors after that.

"I'm trying to remember how it goes in the book," said Dr. Cham, as he walked swiftly through the hall. "That milky fog that swept across the projection. We find that thing." He jiggled a door handle, broke it off. Forged through the doorway and disappeared inside.

"You really get a kick out of beating stuff up, don't you?" said the goat. "Walls, doors." The goat headbutted a wall. The wall shuddered and then laid still.

Then, it was quiet. And black.

The goat stayed put in the bleak hallway, expecting Dr. Cham to flip over a few desks and emerge, ready to move on from the room he'd busted into. But Dr. Cham didn't return, and the goat opted to share a moment with the neglected wreckage left by his neighbors. Not that he could see at all. He could only hear the occasional rustling of the piles of invoices and carbon copy masters and manila envelopes when he shifted his legs.

The ground seemed to buckling right under the goat, as if the heaps of kipple around him were beginning to slide toward his weight. He would be at the center of this whirlpool of elephant documentation. Would he die of papercuts first? Or would he suffocate under the solid burial by office supplies?

A soft light, however, crept up to him. A floating, silver fish. No, it was a—was it scissors? The scissors grew into a shimmering cluster of intelligent bread, each slice choking on glitter. But, no, it was hands. And an Easter hat.

The goat alone in the hallway, meets an apparition.

In another room, Dr. Cham stood under the clear glass silently. The ceiling had abruptly gone transparent, then starlight washed over his pants and jacket. He walked further to the room's center in muted colors, lit as softly as an ancient manuscript in its own box at the museum. More stars, more cotton clusters of fire, unveiled as he came across the floor. And it peeked into view soon enough, he expected it to be larger, but it wasn't.

Earth. Like a painted egg, still fresh. He felt long cello strings sing right up against his spine. How could that be called Peoplemud? Here was a vibrant and grassy lightbulb. The one big ball that had something going for it.

He thought of The Rockettes. Actually, he missed The Rockettes. What a bunch of great dancers. He had yelled something to The Rockettes when he saw them. Something very observant and flattering.

Oh, yes, while The Rockettes were spinning, arm in arm, he had yelled, "Concentric circles!" Which no one else cared to observe.

And this thought was enough to feed Dr. Cham's superiority complex. He wore a goofy smile as he retraced his footsteps. He truthfully felt his genius coming through in such a statement. To realize the simplicity of a circle was his. He reflected on it all the way back to the hallway.

Which I think is great. Adore yourself when you have a second.

The Doctor knows this ghost.

"Oh, right," said the goat. "Your niece. The niece you killed. I'm with ya now."

For just a few moments, they all looked at each other. Just enough time for both Dr. Cham and the goat to think: *Oh, yeah. Hannah causes us a lot of trouble. She's already talking about maple donuts.*

"Does she start talking about maple donuts right away like that?" asked the goat.

"Yes, she does," said the Doctor. "She brings it up to you, then she brings it up to me. She sees a maple donut somewhere—I don't quite remember where."

"Do I see a real maple donut?" Hannah said. "I need a real one."

"Okay, okay," said the goat. "Yeah, I remember: here's where she says that if she gets a real maple donut, she'll become a real person again. Because her real destiny was to own a bakery and you ruined that destiny and now she's trapped as a ghost."

"Hey, that's the truth!" Hannah yelped.

"It's terrible that we must bear through this whole scene again," said the Doctor. "The donuts are immaterial. They should be left out altogether."

"Man, I am having a *hard* time remembering all of this chapter," said the goat. "I don't even remember how to get out of this hallway. I must have read that book like thirty times. Do we blast through a wall? Do we scream until someone finds us?"

"We get Hannah to float through walls and she finds some kind of machine," says Dr. Cham. "I have to write a program— it all works out somehow."

"But, you know what I'm saying?" said the goat. "I forget all the details. Especially the earlier chapters. I mean I can remember the ending perfectly. It's hard to sit through all this. The end is so much better."

Dr. Cham folded his arms and teetered on a heel. "The porcupine." He smiled greedily at the goat.

"Oh, totally. The porcupine is definitely who I want to meet," said the goat. "I wonder what he does with all that money when the book is over."

Dr. Cham nodded respectfully. "I'm very excited to see him wearing slippers."

"Those infernal slippers!" said the goat and he haw-hawed coarsely, a shower of saliva cascading from his jaws.

Hannah's mind rattled, waiting for this nonsense to break for a moment. She tipped her head on its side and the rattle slid along the curve of her cranium. The little noise died away, though, as the back of her head vanished (*fluxed out* is what she called it) and then her head was back again with its little rattle and she caught herself doing that careless moaning again. **HRRRRRR-RRR-OH-RRRR-RRRR.**

"I'm not as into the chunky bacon stuff," said the goat. "I don't see what's so great about it."

Could she speak while moaning? **BON-BON.** With a French moan. **BOHN-BOHN. BOHN-APPE-TEET-OHHHH-RRRR.**

"I know she's harmless, but that sound freaks me out. My hair is **completely** on end."

"Hannah?" said Dr. Cham. "Where are you, child? Come do a good turn for us, my niece."

She was right near them, in and out. And they could hear her cleaning up her voice, bright, speaking like a angel scattering stardust. Yes, the whole maple donut story came out again, and more about the bakery she would own, the muffins and rolls and baguettes.

5. The Theft of the Lottery Captain

And now, Paij-ree's stories of the Lotteries.

On Endertromb, the organist's father invented the lottery. The idea came while he was praying to Digger Dosh.

Digger Dosh is sort of like their God. But ten times scarier. This guy dug an infinitely deep tunnel straight through the planet and came out dead. But he's really not dead. He's really just *one second* behind them. And he eats time.

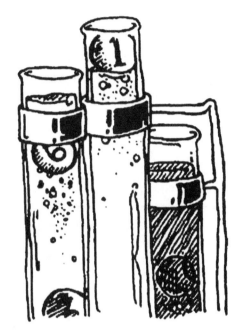

It's kind of complicated because Digger Dosh totally kills people. But I guess if you do what he says, it's not so bad. Maybe I'll talk about it later. It's such a pain to talk about because it's so scary and yet one of my friends actually believes the whole thing. I get kind of choked up—not like I'm crying, more like I'm choking.

Anyway, once while praying, three numbers came to Paij-ree's father.

He then asked his mind, "What are these numbers?"

And his mind played a short video clip of him selling all kinds of numbers. And, for years and years, traveling and selling numbers.

And he asked his brain, "People will buy numbers?"

And his brain said, "If they buy the right three numbers, give them a prize."

At which he imagined himself launching off a ski jump and showering people with presents. No question: he would be an icon.

So he went and did as his brain said and sold numbers. The father's simple lottery consisted of three unique numbers, drawn from a set of 25 numbers.

```ruby
class LotteryTicket

  NUMERIC_RANGE = 1..25

  attr_reader :picks, :purchased

  def initialize( *picks )
    if picks.length != 3
      raise ArgumentError, "three numbers must be picked"
    elsif picks.uniq.length != 3
      raise ArgumentError, "the three picks must be different
numbers"
    elsif picks.detect { |p| not NUMERIC_RANGE === p }
      raise ArgumentError, "the three picks must be numbers
between 1 and 25"
    end
    @picks = picks
    @purchased = Time.now
  end

end
```

Yes, the **LotteryTicket** class contained the three numbers (**@picks**) and the time when the ticket was bought (**@purchased**). The allowed range of numbers (from **one** to **twenty-five**) is kept in the constant **NUMERIC_RANGE**.

The **initialize** method here can have any number of arguments passed in. The **asterisk** in the **picks** argument means that **any arguments will be passed in as an Array**. Having the arguments in an Array means that methods like **uniq** and **detect** can be used on the arguments together.

This class contains two definitions: the method definition (**def**) and an attributes definition (**attr_reader**). Both are **really just method definitions** though.

The **attr_reader** shortcut is identical to writing this Ruby code:

```
class LotteryTicket
  def picks; @picks; end
  def purchased; @purchased; end
end
```

Attributes are wrapper methods for instance variables (such as **@picks**) which can be used **outside of the class itself**. Paij-ree's father wanted to code a machine which could read the numbers and the date of purchase from the ticket. In order to do that, those instance variables must be exposed.

Let's create a random ticket and read back the numbers:

```
ticket = LotteryTicket.new( rand( 25 ) + 1,
          rand( 25 ) + 1, rand( 25 ) + 1 )
p ticket.picks
```

Running the above, I just got: **[23, 14, 20]**. You will get an error if two of the random numbers happen to be identical.

However, I can't change the lottery ticket's picks from outside of the class.

```
ticket.picks = [2, 6, 19]
```

I get an error: **undefined method `picks='**. This is because **attr_reader** only adds a **reader** method, not a writer method. That's fine, though. We don't want the numbers or the date to change.

So, the tickets are *objects*. Instances of the **LotteryTicket** class. Make a ticket with **LotteryTicket.new**. Each ticket has its own **@picks** and its own **@purchased** instance variables.

The lottery captain would need to draw three random numbers at the close of the lottery, so we'll add a convenient class method for generating random tickets.

```
class LotteryTicket
  def self.new_random
    new( rand( 25 ) + 1, rand( 25 ) + 1, rand( 25 ) + 1 )
  end
end
```

Oh, no. But we have that stupid error that pops up if two of the random numbers happen to be identical. If two numbers are the same, the `initialize` throws an **ArgumentError**.

The trick is going to be restarting the method if an error happens. We can use Ruby's **rescue** to handle the error and **retry** to start the method over.

```ruby
class LotteryTicket
  def self.new_random
    new( rand( 25 ) + 1, rand( 25 ) + 1, rand( 25 ) + 1 )
  rescue ArgumentError
    retry
  end
end
```

Better. It may take a couple times for the numbers to fall together right, but it'll happen. The wait will build suspense, huh?

The lottery captain kept a roster of everyone who bought tickets, along with the numbers they drew.

```ruby
class LotteryDraw
  @@tickets = {}
  def LotteryDraw.buy( customer, *tickets )
    unless @@tickets.has_key?( customer )
      @@tickets[customer] = []
    end
    @@tickets[customer] += tickets
  end
end
```

Yal-dal-rip-sip was the first customer.

```ruby
LotteryDraw.buy 'Yal-dal-rip-sip',
LotteryTicket.new( 12, 6, 19 ),
LotteryTicket.new( 5, 1, 3 ),
LotteryTicket.new( 24, 6, 8 )
```

When it came time for the lottery draw, Paij-ree's father (the lottery captain) added a bit of code to randomly select the numbers.

```
class LotteryTicket
  def score( final )
    count = 0
    final.picks.each do |note|
      count +=1 if picks.include? note
    end
    count
  end
end
```

The **score** method compares a **LotteryTicket** against a random ticket, which represents the winning combination. The random ticket is passed in through the **final** variable. The ticket gets one point for every winning number. The point total is returned from the **score** method.

```
irb> ticket = LotteryTicket.new( 2, 5, 19 )
irb> winner = LotteryTicket.new( 4, 5, 19 )
irb> ticket.score( winner )
  => 2
```

You will see how brilliant Paij-ree is, in time. His father commissioned him to finish the lottery for him, while the demand for tickets consumed the lottery captain's daylight hours. Can't you just imagine young Paij-ree in his stuffy suit, snapping a rubber band in his young thumbs at the company meetings where he proposed the final piece of the system? Sure, when he stood up, his dad did all the talking for him, but he flipped on the projector and performed all the hand motions.

```
class << LotteryDraw
  def play
    final = LotteryTicket.new_random
    winners = {}
    @@tickets.each do |buyer, ticket_list|
      ticket_list.each do |ticket|
        score = ticket.score( final )
        next if score.zero?
        winners[buyer] ||= []
        winners[buyer] << [ ticket, score ]
      end
    end
    @@tickets.clear
    winners
  end
end
```

His father's associates were stunned. What was this? (Paij-ree knew this was just another class method definition— they would all feel completely demoralized when he told them so.) They couldn't understand the **double angle bracket** up there! Yes, it was a concatenator, but how is it in the class title?

Infants, thought Paij-ree, although he held everyone of those men in very high esteem. He was just a kid and kids are tough as a brick's teeth.

The **<<** operator allows you to alter the definition of an object. Had Paij-ree simply used **class LotteryDraw**, his **play** method would be a normal instance method. But since he used the **<<** operator, the **play** method will be added directly to the class, as a class method.

When you see **class << obj**, believe in your heart, *I'm adding directly to the definition of obj*.

The budding organ instructor also threw in a tricky syntax worth examining. In the ninth line, a winner has been found.

```
winners[buyer] ||= []
winners[buyer] << [ ticket, score ]
```

The **||=** syntax is a shortcut.

```
winners[buyer] = winners[buyer] || []
```

The **double pipe** is an **or** logic. Set **winners[buyer]** equal to **winners[buyer]** or, if **winners[buyer]** is nil, set it to **[]**. This shortcut is a little strange, but if you can really plant it in your head, it's a nice time-saver. You're just making sure a variable is set before using it.

```
irb> LotteryDraw.play.each do |winner, tickets|
irb>   puts winner + "won on " + tickets.length + " ticket(s)!"
irb>   tickets.each do |ticket, score|
irb>     puts "\t" + ticket.picks.join( ', ' ) + ": " + score
irb>   end
irb> end

Gram-yol won on 2 ticket(s)!
    25, 14, 33: 1
    12, 11, 29: 1
Tarker-azain won on 1 ticket(s)!
    13, 15, 29: 2
Bramlor-exxon won on 1 ticket(s)!
    2, 6, 14: 1
```

But these salad days were not to continue for Paij-ree and his father. His father often neglected to launder his uniform and contracted a moss disease on his shoulders. The disease gradually stole his equilibrium and his sense of direction.

His father still futilely attempted to keep the business running. He spiraled through the city, sometimes tumbling leg-over-leg down the cobbled stone, most often slowly feeling the walls, counting bricks to the math parlors and coachmen stations, where he would thrust tickets at the bystanders, who hounded him and slapped him away with long, wet beets. Later, Paij-ree would find him in a corner, his blood running into the city drains alongside the juices of the dark, splattered beets, which juice weaseled its way up into his veins and stung and clotted and glowed fiercely like a congested army of brake lights fighting their way through toll bridges.

A Word About Accessors (Because I Love You and I Hope For Your Success and My Hair is On End About This and Dreams Really Do Come True)

Earlier, I mentioned that **attr_reader** adds **reader** methods, but not **writer** methods.

```
irb> ticket = LotteryTicket.new
irb> ticket.picks = 3
NoMethodError: undefined method `picks=' for
#<LotteryTicket:0xb7d49110>
```

Which is okay in this case, since Paij-ree's father didn't want the numbers to be changed after the ticket was bought. If we were interested in having instance variables which had **both readers and writers**, we would use **attr_accessor**.

```
class LotteryTicket
  attr_accessor :picks, :purchased
end
```

Which is exactly the same as this lengthier code:

```
class LotteryTicket
  def picks;            @picks;            end
  def picks=(var);      @picks = var;      end
  def purchased;        @purchased;        end
  def purchased=(var);  @purchased = var;  end
end
```

Holy cats! Look at those writer methods for a moment. They are the methods named **picks=** and **purchased=**. These methods **intercept outside assignment** to instance variables. Usually you will just let **attr_reader** or **attr_accessor** (or even perhaps **attr_writer**) do the work for you. Other times you may want to put a guard at the door yourself, checking variables in closer detail.

```ruby
class SkatingContest
  def the_winner; @the_winner; end
  def the_winner=( name )
    unless name.respond_to? :to_str
      raise ArgumentError, "The winner's name must be a String,
        not a math problem or a list of names or any of that
        business."
    end
    @the_winner = name
  end
end
```

Most of the time you won't use this. But, as we move along through your lessons, you'll find that Ruby has lots of escape hatches and alley ways you can sneak into and hack code into. I'm also preparing you for metaprogramming, which, if you can smell that dragon, is ominously near.

Paij-ree was an enterprising young Endertromaltoek. He hammered animal bones into long, glistening trumpets with deep holes that were plugged by corks the musicians banded to their fingers. Sure, he only sold three of those units, but he was widely reviled as a freelance scholar, a demonic one, for he was of a poorer class and the poor only ever acquired their brilliance through satanic practice. Of course, they were right, indeed, he did have a bargain with the dark mages, whom he kept appointments with annually, enduring torturous hot springs, bathing as they chanted spells.

He adored his father, even as his father deteriorated into but a gyroscope. He idolized the man's work and spent his own small earnings playing the lottery. He loved to watch the numerals, each painted upon hollow clay balls, rise in the *robloch* (which is any fluid, pond or spill that has happened to withstand the presence of ghosts), the great bankers tying them together on a silver string, reading them in order.

Even today, Paij-ree paints the scenes with crude strokes of black ink on sheets of aluminum foil. It is very touching to see him caught up in the preciousness of his memory, but I don't know exactly why he does it on aluminum foil. His drawings rip too easily. Paij-ree himself gets mixed up and

Another Excerpt from *The Scarf Eaters*
(from *Chapter VIII: Sky High.*)

"I know you," said Brent. "And I know your timelines. You couldn't have done this Flash piece."

"So, you're saying I'm predictable?" said Deborah. She opened her hands and the diced potatoes stumbled like little, drunk sea otters happily into the open crockpot.

"You're very linear," said Brent. He took up a mechanical pencil, held it straight before his eyes, gazing tightly at it before replacing it in the pencil holder on the counter. "Do you even know how to load a scene? How to jump frames? This movie I saw was all over the place, Deb."

She heaped five knit scarves and a single bandanna into the slow cooker and set it on high. She closed the lid, leaving her hand resting upon it.

"What is it about this movie?" Deborah asked. "You go to Flash sites all the time. You played the Elf Snowball game for two seconds, it didn't interest you. You didn't care for Elf Bowling games even. And you weren't even phased by that Hit The Penguin flash game. Elf versus Penguin? Don't even ask!

"Now this movie comes along and you can't get a grip." She walked over and sidled up next to him. "Yo, bro, it's me. Deborah. What happened when you saw that movie?"

"Everything," said Brent, his eyes reflecting a million worlds. "And: nothing. It opened with a young girl riding upon a wild boar. She was playing harmonica. The harmonica music washed in and out, uneasy, unsure. But she rode naturally, as if it wasn't anything of a big deal to ride a wild boar. And with Flash, riding a wild boar really isn't a big deal."

Deborah unclasped her bracelet and set it on the counter by the crockpot.

"The bottom of the movie started to break up, an ink puddle formed. The boar reared up, but his legs gave way to the all the dark, sputtering ink."

"Dark clouds converged. Hardcore music started to play. Secret agents came out of the clouds. CIA guys and stuff. The animation simply rocked.

"And then, at the very end of the movie, these words fade upon the screen. In white, bold letters."

"Sky high," said Deborah.

"How did you know?" Brent's lip quivered. Could she be trusted?

"There is no room left in the world," she said. "No room for Scarf Eaters, no room for you and I. Here, take my hand."

will serve you crumbcake right off of some of this art, even after it has been properly framed. So many things about him are troubling and absurd and downright wretched.

The disease spread over his father's form and marshy weeds covered his father's hands and face. The moss pulled his spine up into a rigid uprightness. So thick was the growth over his head that he appeared to wear a shrub molded into a bowler's hat. He also called himself by a new name—**Quos**—and he healed the people he touched, leaving a pile of full-blooded, greenly-cheeked villages in his wake as he traveled the townships. Many called him The Mossiah and wept on his feet, which wet the buds and caused him to weed into the ground. This made him momentarily angry, he harshly jogged his legs to break free and thrashed his fists wildly in the sky, bringing down a storm of lightning shards upon these pitiful.

Paij-ree was apart from the spiritual odysseys of his father (in fact, thought the man dead), so he only saw the decay of the lottery without its captain present. Here is where Paij-ree went to work, reviving the dead lottery of his family.

Gambling with Fewer Fingers

The city was crowded with people who had lost interest in the lottery. The weather had really worn everyone down as well. Such terrible rain flooding their cellars. The entire city was forced to move up one story. You'd go to put the cap back on your pen and you'd ruin the pen, since the cap was already full of slosh. Everyone was depleted, many people drowned.

Paij-ree found himself wasting his days in a quadruple bunkbed, the only furniture that managed to stay above sea level. He slept on the top bed. The third bed up was dry as well, so he let a homeless crater gull nest upon it. The gull didn't need the whole bed, so Paij-ree also kept his calculators and pencils down there.

At first, these were very dark times for both of them, and they insisted on remaining haggard at all times. Paij-ree became obsessed with his fingernails, kept them long and pristine, while the rest of him deteriorated under a suit of hair. In the company of Paij-ree, the crater gull learned his own eccentricity and plucked all the feathers on the right side of his body. He looked like a cutaway diagram.

They learned to have happier times. Paij-ree carved a flute from the wall with his nails and played it often. Mostly he played his relaxed ballads during the daytime. In the evening, they pounded the wall and shook the bed frame in time to his songs. The gull went nuts when he played a certain four notes and he looped this section repeatedly, watching the gull swoop and circle in ecstasy. Paij-ree could hardly keep his composure over the effect the little tune had and he couldn't keep it together, fell all apart, slobbering and horse-giggling.

Paij-ree called the gull *Eb-F-F-A*, after that favorite song.

Friendship can be a very good catalyst for progress. A friend can find traits in you that no one else can. It's like they searched your person and somehow came up with five full sets of silverware you never knew were there. And even though that friend may not understand why you had these utensils concealed, it's still a great feat, worth honoring.

While *Eb-F-F-A* didn't find silverware, he did find something else. A pile of something else. Since Paij-ree was stranded on the quadruple bed, the gull would scout around for food. One day, he flew down upon a barrel, floating over where the tool shed had been. *Eb-F-F-A* walked on top of the barrel, spinning it back to Paij-ree's house and they cracked it open, revealing Paij-ree's lost collection of duck bills.

Yes, real duck bills. (*Eb-F-F-A* was esophagizing his squawks, remaining calm, sucking beads of sweat back into his forehead—ducks were not *of his chosen feather*, but still in the species.) Paij-ree clapped gleefully, absolutely, he had intended to shingle his house with these, they could have deflected a bit of the torrent. Probably not much, nothing to cry about.

And the roof glue was at the barrel's bottom and they were two enterprising bunkmates with time to kill, so they made a raft from the previously-quacked lip shades. And off they were to the country! Stirring through a real mess of city and soup. How strange it was to hit a beach and find out it was just the old dirt road passed Toffletown Junction.

In the country, they sold. It was always a long walk to the next plantation, but there would be a few buyers up in the mansion ("Welcome to The Mansion Built on Beets", they'd say or, "The Mansion Built on Cellophane Substitutes—don't you know how harmful real cellophane can be?") And one of the families wrapped up some excess jelly and ham in some cellophane for the two travelers. And they almost died one day later because of it.

Then, when the heat came and, as the first countryside lottery was at nigh, a farmer called to them from his field, as he stood by his grazing cow. Paij-ree and *Eb-F-F-A* wandered out to him, murmuring to each other as to whether they should offer him the Wind-Beaten Ticket Special or whether he might want to opt in to winning Risky Rosco's Original Homestyle Country Medallion.

But the farmer waved them down as he approached, "No, put your calculators and probability wheels away. It's for my grazledon." He meant his cow. The Endertromb version: twice as much flesh, twice as meaty, doesn't produce milk, produces paper plates. Still, it grazes.

"Your grazledon (poh-kon-ic) wants a lucky ticket?" asked Paij-ree.

"He saw you two and got real excited," said the farmer. "He doesn't know numbers, but he understands luck a bit. He almost got hit by a doter plane one day and, when I found him, he just gave shrug. It was like he said, 'Well, I guess that worked out okay.'"

"The whole (shas-op) lottery is numer-(ig-ig)-ic," said Paij-ree. "Does he know (elsh) notes? My eagle knows (losh) notes." Paij-ree whistled at the crater gull, who cooed back a sustained *D*.

The farmer couldn't speak to his grazledon's tonal awareness, so Paij-ree sent the gull to find out (*D-D-D-A-D, go-teach-the-grazle*) while he hacked some notes into his calculator.

```ruby
class AnimalLottoTicket
  # A list of valid notes.
  NOTES = [:Ab, :A, :Bb, :B, :C, :Db, :D, :Eb, :E, :F, :Gb, :G]

  # Stores the three picked notes and a purchase date.
  attr_reader :picks, :purchased

  # Creates a new ticket from three chosen notes.  The three notes
  # must be unique notes.
  def initialize( note1, note2, note3 )
    if [note1, note2, note3].uniq!
      raise ArgumentError, "the three picks must be different notes"
    elsif picks.detect { |p| not NOTES.include? p }
      raise ArgumentError, "the three picks must be notes in the
chromatic scale."
    end
    @picks = picks
    @purchased = Time.now
  end

  # Score this ticket against the final draw.
  def score( final )
    count = 0
    final.picks.each do |note|
      count +=1 if picks.include? note
    end
    count
  end

  # Constructor to create a random AnimalLottoTicket
  def self.new_random
    new( NOTES[ rand( NOTES.length ) ],
         NOTES[ rand( NOTES.length ) ],
         NOTES[ rand( NOTES.length ) ] )
  rescue ArgumentError
    retry
  end
end
```

No need for the animal's tickets to behave drastically different from the traditional tickets. The `AnimalLottoTicket` class is internally different, but exposes the same methods seen in the original `LotteryTicket` class. The `score` method is even identical to the `score` method from the old `LotteryTicket` class.

Instead of using a class variable to store the musical note list, they're stored in a constant called `AnimalLottoTicket::NOTES`. Variables change and the note list shouldn't change. Constants are designed to stay the same. You can still change the constant, but you'll have to be tricky or Ruby will speak up.

```
irb> AnimalLottoTicket::NOTES = [:TOOT, :TWEET, :BLAT]
(irb):3: warning: already initialized constant NOTES
  => [:TOOT, :TWEET, :BLAT]
```

The gull came back with the grazledon, his name was Merphy, he was thrilled to play chance, he puffed his face dreamily, whistled five and six notes in series, they all held his collar, pulled him close to the calculator and let him breathe three notes, then they choked the bedosh outta him until his ticket was printed and everything was nicely cataloged inside `@@tickets['merphy']`. Thank you, see ya at the draw!

So, the fever of the lottery became an epidemic among the simple minds of the animals. Paij-ree saved his costs, used the same `LotteryDraw` class he'd used in the corporate environment of the lottery from his childhood. And soon enough, the animals were making their own music and their own maps and films.

"What about The Originals?" I asked Paij-ree. "They must have hated your animals!"

But he winced sourly and pinched his forehead. "I am an Original. You as well. Do we (ae-o) hate any of them?"

Not too long after the lottery ended, Paij-ree felt the crater gull *Eb-F-F-A* lighting upon his shoulder, which whistled an urgent and sad *C-Eb-D C-A-Eb*. These desperate notes sent an organ roll of chills straight through Paij-ree. Had the King God of Potted Soil, Our Beloved Topiary, **the Mossiah Quos**, Literal Father of That Man Who Would Be My Daughter's Organ Instructor—had he truly come to his end? How could this be? Could the great arbors no longer nourish him and guide the moist crosswinds to him? Or did his own spindly lichen hedge up his way and grow against his breathing?

You never mind, went the tune of the gull. *He has deteriorated and weakened and fallen in the lit door of your home cottage. His tendrils needing and crying for the day to not end. For the sun to stay fixed and wide and attentive.*

Plor-ian, the house attendant, kept the pitchers coming and Quos stayed well watered until Paij-ree arrived to survey the decaying buds of soft plant and the emerging face of his father, the lottery captain. His skin deeply pocked like an overly embroidered pillow. Great shoots springing from his sleeves now curled back with lurching thirst.

Paij-ree combed back the longer stems around his father's eyes and those coming from the corners of his mouth. While I'd like to tell you that Paij-ree's tears rolled down his sleeves and into the pours of his father, rejuvenating and restoring the grassy gentleman: I cannot say this.

Rather, Paij-ree's tears rolled down his sleeves and into the creaking clapboard floor, nourishing the vile weeds, energizing the dark plant matter, which literally leapt through the floor at night and strangled Our Quos. Yank, pull, crack. And that was his skull.

So Paij-ree could never be called Wert-ree or Wert-plo after that.

6. Them What Make the Rules

Hannah leapt back from the wall and clenched down on her fingers.

"This is the wall," said Dr. Cham. "The Originals are in there. My child, can you lead us to the observation deck?"

"You expect us to go up against those guys?" asked the goat. "They're mad as koalas. But these koalas have lasers!"

"We prevail, though," said Dr. Cham. "You and I know this."

"Okay, well I'm muddled on that point," said the goat. "Do we really win? Or could we be thinking about *Kramer vs. Kramer*? Does Dustin Hoffman win or do we win?"

"No. No. No. No." Hannah hovered and dragged her legs along the wall nervously. "There is a man with a huge face in there!"

"Mr. Face," said the Doctor. "He is the original face."

"He didn't see me," said Hannah and moaned. **HOMA-HOMA-ALLO-ALLO.**

She made that hollow weeping through the crumbling mouseholes and the freezer gateways, fluxing in and out, causing the video checkpoints to hiss and the wall panels to brace themselves and fall silent. The three passed through two levels of frayed security and emerged in the observation deck overlooking the cargo bay.

Klon Ooper. Corwood. Mr. Face. Vonblisser. The Originals.

"The last living among The Originals," said Dr. Cham. "Are you alright with this, Hannah?" Which she didn't hear in any way, as her eyes laid fixed on the legendary creatures.

"Look at them," said the goat. "These guys wrote the rule books, Doctor. We owe everything to these guys."

"What about God?" said Dr. Cham.

"I don't really know," said the goat. "Hannah probably knows better than any of us about that."

Hannah said nothing. She only really knew one other ghost and that was her Post-Decease Mediator, Jamie Huft. Who didn't seem to have any answers for her and required questions to be submitted in writing with a self-addressed stamped envelope included. Hannah hadn't gotten the ball rolling on that P.O. Box yet.

"We must be up in the mountains," said the goat. "Look out at that blackness."

"I saw another deck like this down by where we found Hannah," said Dr. Cham. "Down closer to your living area. You should take time to search for it. It's very peaceful there. You can see Earth and the seven seas."

"The seven seas?" The goat wondered if that was near The Rockettes. He'd read his share of material on precision dancing and he'd seen that line of legs, mincing across the stage like a big, glitsy rototiller.

Hannah stirred to life.

Hannah panics. Maple donuts are within reach.

They couldn't hear them, but they saw their slides.

And none of the three spoke when The Originals flicked off the slide projector and boarded a very slender rocket ship and cleanly exploded through a crevice in the cargo bay roof.

"Oh, boy," said the goat.

"What?" said Hannah.

"You're going to die," said the goat.

Dr. Cham looked over the controls in front of them, a long panel of padded handles and green screens.

"I'm already dead. I'm a ghost."

The goat looked down at the Doctor, who was rummaging under the control panel. "Okay, well if your uncle isn't going to have a talk with you, I'm going to make things very clear. There's a good chance these guys are going to build a bomb. And you see how I'm fidgeting? You see how my knees are wobbling?"

"Yeah."

"Yeah, that's how real this is, kid. I don't remember anything from that *confounded book* except that these guys are building a bomb that can blow up the ghost world. Because once the ghost world's gone, then Digger Dosh gets his one second back. It's a trade they've worked out. Hell, it's sick stuff, that's all you need to know."

"But I'm dead."

"Okay, well, we're talking, aren't we? You can talk, so are you dead?" The goat shook his head. "I wish I could remember if we win or if it was Dustin Hoffman."

Hannah cried. "Why do I have to die again?" She wailed and her legs fell into flux and she sunk into the floor. **MOH-MOHHH-MAO-MAOOO.**

Dr. Cham had forcibly yanked on a plush handle, which unlocked and slid open like a breadbox. He reached his hands inside and found a keyboard firmly bolted deep inside.

"That's it," he said and pulled up **irb**, which appeared on a display to the left of his concealed typing. He checked the Ruby version.

```
irb> RUBY_VERSION
  => "1.9.3"
```

Ruby was up-to-date. What else could he do? Scanning **constants** and **class_variables** was pointless. The only reason that had worked with the **Elevator** class was because someone had left **irb** running with their classes still loaded.

He had just loaded this **irb**, so no special classes were available yet. He had to find some classes. He started by loading the **rbconfig** file to get an idea of what Ruby's settings were.

```
irb> require 'rbconfig'
  => true
irb> RbConfig::CONFIG
  => {"abs_srcdir"=>"$(ac_abs_srcdir)",
"sitedir"=>"bay://Ruby/lib/site_ruby", ... }
```

Too much information to sort through there. The **RbConfig::CONFIG** constant is a Hash that contains every environment setting used to setup Ruby. You can find the operating system name at **RbConfig::CONFIG['host_os']**. The directory where core Ruby libraries are stored can be found at **RbConfig::CONFIG['rubylibdir']**. Ruby programs can store helper files at **RbConfig::CONFIG['datadir']**.

What Dr. Cham really needed, though, was a list of all the libraries that aren't core Ruby libraries. Libraries which were installed by

The Originals or whoever manned this console. He checked a few global variables for this information.

```
irb> $"
  => ["irb.rb", "e2mmap.rb", "irb/init.rb", ... "rbconfig.rb"]
irb> $:
  => ["bay://Ruby/lib/site_ruby/1.9", "bay://Ruby/lib/site_
ruby/1.9/i686-unknown",
      "bay://Ruby/lib/site_ruby", "bay://Ruby/lib/1.9",
      "bay://Ruby/lib/1.9/i686-unknown"]
```

Aha, good. Dr. Cham stroked his beard and looked over his **irb** session. The **$"** global variable contains an Array of every library which has been loaded with **require**. Most of these libraries had been loaded by **irb**. He had loaded **'rbconfig.rb'** earlier, though.

The **$:** global variable, which can also be accessed as **$LOAD_PATH**, contains a list of all the directories which Ruby will check when you try to load a file with **require**. When Dr. Cham ran **require 'rbconfig'**, Ruby checked each directory in order.

```
bay://Ruby/lib/site_ruby/1.9/rbconfig.rb
bay://Ruby/lib/site_ruby/1.9/i686-unknown/rbconfig.rb (*)
bay://Ruby/lib/site_ruby/rbconfig.rb
bay://Ruby/lib/1.9/rbconfig.rb
bay://Ruby/lib/1.9/i686-unknown/rbconfig.rb
```

The second path was where Ruby ended up finding the rbconfig.rb file. Dr. Cham guessed that the first five paths were **absolute paths.** These were paths to directories on a drive called **bay.** Absolute paths may vary on your system. On Windows, absolute paths will start with a drive letter. On Linux, absolute paths start with a slash.

The goat had peeked his head around Dr. Cham and was watching all these instructions transpire, as he licked his lips to keep his salivations from running all over the monitors and glossy buttons. He had been interjecting a few short cheers (along the lines of: *No, not that* or *Yes, yes, right* or *Okay, well, your choice*), but now he was fully involved, recommending code, "Try **require 'setup'** or, no, try **3 * 5**. Make sure that basic math works."

"Of course the math works," said Dr. Cham. "Let me be, I need to find some useful classes."

"It's a basic sanity test," said the goat. "Just try it. Do **3 * 5** and see what comes up."

Dr. Cham caved.

```
irb> 3 * 5
  => 15
```

"Okay, great! We're in business!" The goat tossed his furry face about in glee.

Dr. Cham patted the goat's head, "Well done. We can continue."

```
irb> Dir.chdir( "bay://Ruby/lib/site_ruby/1.9/" )
  => 0
irb> Dir["./*.{rb}"]
  => ['endertromb.rb', 'mindreader.rb', 'wishmaker.rb']
```

Dr. Cham had use **chdir** to change the current working directory over the first path listed in **$LOAD_PATH**. This first path in **site_ruby** is a common place to store custom classes.

Here were the three legendary classes that my daughter's organ instructor had inscribed for me earlier in this chapter. And, Dr. Cham, having read this selfsame chapter, recognized these three pieces of the system immediately.

The **Endertromb** class which contained the mysteries of this planet's powers. The **MindReader** class which, upon scanning the minds of its inhabitants, read each mind's contents. And, finally, the crucial **WishMaker** class which powered the granting of ten-letter wishes, should the wish ever find its way to the core of Endertromb.

"How about **4 * 56 + 9**?" asked the goat. "We don't know if it can do compound expressions."

"I've got the **MindReader** right here," said Dr. Cham. "And I have the **WishMaker** here next to it. This planet can read minds. And this planet can make wishes. Now, let's see if it can do both at the same time."

7. Them What Live the Dream

While The Originals' craft had long disappeared, Dr. Cham frantically worked away at the computer built into the control panel up in the observation deck. Hannah had disappeared into the floor (or perhaps those little sparks along the ground were still wisps of her paranormal presence!) and the goat amicably watched Dr. Cham hack out a Ruby module.

```ruby
require 'endertromb'
module WishScanner
  def scan_for_a_wish
    wish = self.read.detect do |thought|
      thought.index( 'wish: ' ) == 0
    end
    wish.gsub( 'wish: ', '' )
  end
end
```

"What's your plan?" asked the goat. "It seems like I could have solved this problem in like three lines."

"This **Module** is the new **WishScanner** technology," he said. "The scanner only picks up a wish if it starts with the word **wish** and a colon and a space. That way the planet doesn't fill up with every less-than-ten-letter word that appears in people's heads."

"Why don't you just use a class?" asked the goat.

"Because a **Module** is simpler than a class. It's basically just a storage facility for methods. It keeps a group of methods together. You can't create new objects from a module."

"But aren't you going to want a **WishScanner** object, so you can actually use it?" said the goat, appalled.

"I'm going to mix it into the **MindReader**," said Dr. Cham. And he did.

```ruby
require 'mindreader'
class MindReader
  include WishScanner
end
```

"Now, the **WishScanner** module is mixed in to the **MindReader**," said Dr. Cham. "I can call the **scan_for_a_wish** method on any **MindReader** object."

"So, it's a mixin," said the goat. "The **WishScanner** mixin."

"Yes, any module which is introduced into a class with **include** is a mixin to that class. If you go back and look at the **scan_for_a_wish** method, you'll see that it calls a **self.read** method. I just have to make sure that whatever class I'm mixing **WishScanner** into has a **read** method. Otherwise, an error will be thrown."

"That seems really weird that the mixin requires certain methods that it doesn't already have. It seems like it should work by itself."

Dr. Cham looked up from the keyboard at the goat. "Well, it's sort of like your video collection. None of your video cassettes work unless they are put in a machine that uses video cassettes. They depend on each other. A mixin has some basic requirements, but once a class meets those requirements, you can add all this extra functionality in."

"Hey, that's cool," said the goat.

"You read the book thirty times and you didn't pick that up?" asked Dr. Cham.

"You're a much better teacher in person," said the goat. "I really didn't think I was going to like you very much."

"I completely understand," said the Doctor. "This is much more real than the cartoons make it seem."

```ruby
require 'wishmaker'
reader = MindReader.new
wisher = WishMaker.new
loop do
  wish = reader.scan_for_a_wish
  if wish
    wisher.grant( wish )
  end
end
```

Irb sat and looped on the screen. It'll do that until you hit Control-C. But Dr. Cham let it churn away. Looping endlessly, scanning the mind waves for a proper wish.

And Dr. Cham readied his wish. At first, he thought immediately of a **stallion**. To ride bareback over the vales of Sedna. But he pulled the thought back, his wish hadn't been formed properly. A stallion was useless in pursuing The Originals, so he closed his eyes again, bit his lip and he thought to himself: `wish: whale`.

Last Whale to Peoplemud

The blocky, sullen whale appeared down at the castle entrance, where Hannah was bashing on a rosebud with her hand. She whacked at it with a fist, but it only stayed perfect and pleasant and crisp against the solid blue sky of Endertromb.

"I'm bored," she said to the whale. **BOHR-BOHR-OHRRRRRR.**

"OK," said the whale, deep and soft. As the word slid along his massive tongue, its edges chipped off and the word slid out polished and worn in a bubble by his mouth's corner.

"I always have to die," said the young ghost. "People always kill me."

The whale fluttered his short fins, which hung at useless distance from the ground. So, he pushed himself toward her with his tail. Scooting over patches of grass.

"People kill, so who do they kill?" said the girl. "Me. They kill me every time."

The whale made it to within three meters of the girl, where he towered like a great war monument that represents enough dead soldiers to actually steal a lumbering step towards you. And now, the whale rested his tail and, exhausted by the climb thus far, let his eyelids fall shut and became a gently puffing clay mountain, his shadow rich and doubled-up all around the hardly visible Hannah.

But another shadow combined, narrow and determined. Right behind her, the hand came on to her shoulder, and the warm ghost inside the hand touched her sleeve.

"How did you get down here?" said the girl.

Dr. Cham sat right alongside her and the goat walked around and stood in front.

"Listen to us," said Dr. Cham. "We've got to follow this mangy pack of ne'er-do-wells to the very end, Hannah. And to nab them, we need your faithful assistance!"

"I'm scared," cried Hannah.

"You're not scared," said the goat. "Come on. You're a terrifying little phantom child."

"Well," she said. "I'm a little bored."

Dr. Cham bent down on a knee, bringing his shaggy presence toward the ground, his face just inches from hers. "If you come with us, if you can trust what we know, then we can bag this foul troupe. Now, you say your destiny is to be a baker. I won't dispute that. You have every right on Earth— and Endertromb, for that matter—to become a baker. Say, if you didn't become a baker, that would be a great tragedy. Who's going to take care of all those donuts if you don't?"

She shrugged. "That's what I've been saying."

"You're right," said the Doctor. "You've been saying it from the start." He looked up to the sky, where the wind whistled peacefully despite its forceful piercing by The Originals' rocket ship. "If your destiny is to be a baker, then mine is to stop all this, to end the mayhem that is just beginning to boil. And hear me, child—hear how sure and solid my voice becomes when I say this—I ended your life, I bear sole responsibility for your life as an apparition, but I will get it back. It's going to take more than a donut, but you will have a real childhood. I promise you."

On the wished whale... away...

Sure, it took a minute for the goat to cut his wish down to ten letters, but he was shortly on his way, following the same jet streams up into the sky, up toward Dr. Cham and his ghost niece Hannah. Up toward the villanous animal combo pak called The Originals. Up toward The Rockettes.

And Digger Dosh bludgeoned and feasted on each second they left behind them.

Downtown

Oblivious to their involvement in the expansive plan of The Originals, both the tall fox and the much shorter fox had wandered right into the red alert zone, the city Wixl. I desire a spatula to scoop them aside with, shuffle them off to the coast near the beach hatcheries, hide them in piles of fish eggs, hold down their pointy ears, concealing their luxurious hides. And above them I would stand, casting an unmoving shadow, holding my rifle aloof.

I can't. I have you to teach. I have to groom and care for myself. The lightbulbs upstairs need changing. A free pack of halogen lightbulbs just showed up out of the mail. Somebody out there is obviously trying to get me to use them. So I'm going to screw 'em in. And just stand there, casting an unmoving shadow, holding my rifle aloof.

Should that shadow be nice and defined, then I'll keep 'em.

1. If I Were Looking For a Vehicle

Sitting for a moment.

I like seeing these two out in the wild. They got pretty bored here in the studio. They started making up weird slogans and stuff. They had some phrase they kept repeating, forming fixations upon. You can't be exposed to all that contrived fox nonsense.

Let's just say: I am really trying my best to keep things collegiate. Having never attended college, I can't well say if every passage written chimes right with the stringent criteria which academia demands. I have university friends aplenty, some who tour the globe in their pursuits, and I try to inflect my voice with just their blend of high culture.

Sometimes I applaud myself for going beyond the work of my educated friends—only in quiet corridors, we never butt heads publicly—because *I have actually subscribed* to a school of thought while they are still in their books, turning and turning.

I am a preeventualist. I have dabbled in it long enough and am glad to come forth with it. Inevitably, some of you have already started mining this book for Marxist symbology. I am sad to kill those interpretations, but I believe any nihilist conclusions you've drawn will still hold up under scrutiny.

Anyway, I'll drop the rhetoric. I only mention preeventualism because, aside from being a refreshing and easy alternative to the post-modernism we're born with, *this* meta-cult offers a free lost-and-found service for the residents of Wixl.

```
require 'open-uri'
open( "http://preeventualist.org/lost" ) do |lost|
  puts lost.read
end
```

I have no way of alerting the foxes to this service. And I'm sure it's too soon for their truck to be listed. Still, the good intentions are here.

If you're connected to the Internet, the above Ruby should have downloaded the web page from the Internet and printed it to the screen. In a message resembling this:

```
            THE PREEVENTUALIST'S LOSING AND FINDING REGISTRY
         (a free service benefiting the ENLIGHTENED who have been LIGHTENED)
                                    ---
                 updates are made daily, please check back!
                                    ---
                     this service is commissioned and
                  subsidized in part by The Ashley Raymond
                              Youth Study Clan
                                    ...
                   all seals and privileges have been filed
              under the notable authorship of Perry W. L. Von Frowling,
       Magistrate Polywaif of Dispossession.  Also, Seventh Straight Winner
                 of the esteemed Persistent Beggar's Community Cup.
                                    ...


ABOUT THE REGISTRY
==================
Hello, if you are new, please stay with us.  A brief explanation of our service will
follow.  First, a bit of important news from our beloved magistrate.  (The kids call
him Uncle Von Guffuncle. Tehe!)

IMPORTANT NEWS
==============
/ 15 April 2005 /
hi, big news.  we were on channel 8 in wixl and ordish.  cory saw it.  i was on and
jerry mathers was on.  if you didn't see it, e-mail cory.  he tells it the best.  all
i can say is those aren't MY hand motions!! (joke for people who watch channel 8.)
thanks harry and whole channel 8 news team!!
                                - perry

/ 07 April 2005 /
we're all sifting through the carpet here at hq, but if you could all keep an eye out
for caitlin's clipboard, she's too quiet of a gal to post it and i know that it's
REALLY important to her.  she had a few really expensive panoramic radiographs of her
husband's underbite clipped to a few irreplacable photos of her husband in a robocop
costume back when the underbite was more prominent.  she says (to me), "they'll know
what i mean when they see them."  i don't know what that means.  :(

i've checked: * the front desk * the hall * the waiting area * the bathroom * the candy
closet * the big tv area * the lunch counter * the disciples room * gaff's old room
(the one with the painting of the cherry tree) * the server room * staircase.  i'll
update this as i find more rooms.
                                - love, perry

/ 25 Feb 2005 /
server went down at 3 o'clock.  i'm mad as you guys.  gaff is downstairs and he'll
be down there until he gets it fixed. :0 -- UPDATE: it's fixed, back in bizz!!
                                - perry

/ 23 Feb 2005 /
i know there's a lot of noise today.  stanley bros circus lost twelve llamas and a
trailer and a bunch of Masterlocks and five tents.  they're still finding lost stuff.
pls keep your heads, i need everyone's help.  these entertainers have _nothing_.  i
mean it.  i gave a guy a purple sticker today (it's just something i like to do as a
kind gesture) and he practically slept on it and farmed the ingredients for pizza sauce
on it.  they are on rock bottom.

so please donate.  i know we don't have paypal or anything.  so if you want to donate,
just post that you found something (a children's bike, a month of perishable canned
goods) and that it has the circus people's names written on it or something.
                                - great, perry

/ 15 Nov 2004 /
preeventualist's day sale.  if you lose something today, you get to pick one free
item (of $40 value or less) from the house of somebody who found something.  we're
having so much fun with this!!  this is EXACTLY how i got my rowing machine last year
and i LOVE IT!!
                                - perry
```

I think the Youth Study Clan is doing a great job with this service. It's a little hokey and threadbare, but if it can get animals to stop using their instinctive means of declaring ownership, then hats off.

Still, a preeventualist youth group? How can that be? You've got to at least *flirted with real cynicism* before you can become a preeventualist. And you definitely can't attend school. So, I don't know.

Going back to the list of instructions from the Preeventualist's Losing and Finding Registry.

```
USING THE L&F SERVER
====================
The L&F is a free service.  The acts of losing and finding are essential qualities in
building a preeventualist lifestyle.  We hope to accommodate your belief.

We do not use HTML, in order to simplify our work here.  Our guys are already working
fifteen hour days.  (Thanks, Terk!!  Thanks, Horace!!)

You may search our service for your lost items.  Or you may add your lost (or found)
item to our registry.  This is done by typing the proper address into your browser.

SEARCHING
=========
To search for lost items, use the following address:

  http://preeventualist.org/lost/search?q={search word}

You may replace {search word} with your search term.  For example, to search for "cup":

  http://preeventualist.org/lost/search?q=cup

You will be given a list of cups which have been lost or found.

If you want to search for only lost cups or only found cups, use the `searchlost' and
`searchfound' pages:

  http://preeventualist.org/lost/searchlost?q=cup
```

I'm not playing games. I know where the truck is. Really, I'm not teasing you. I'll show you in just a sec. I'm just saying, look at the foxes:

Hummmmm.

They are helpless. And yet, here is this great tool. A possible key to getting out of this mess. I just want to poke around, see if there are any clues here.

```
require 'open-uri'

# Searching all found items containing the word `truck'.
open(
  "http://preeventualist.org/lost/searchfound?q=truck"
) do |truck|
  puts truck.read
end
```

I'm not seeing anything about the tall fox's truck in this list. That's okay. The foxes are out of it anyway. We have some time.

You've learned a very simple technique for retrieving a web page from the Internet. The code uses the **OpenURI** library, which was written by one of my favorite Rubyists, Akira Tanaka. He's simplified reading from the Internet so that it's identical to reading a file from your computer.

In a previous chapter, we stored your diabolical ideas in a text file. You read these files in Ruby using **open**.

```
require 'open-uri'

# Opening an idea file from a folder on your computer.
open( "folder/idea-about-hiding-lettuce-in-the-church-
chairs.txt" ) do |idea|
  puts idea.read
end
```

Files are **input-output objects**. You can read and write to a file. In Ruby, all IO (input-output) objects have **read** and **write** methods. The **open** method slides an IO object **down the chute** into a block for your use. IO is your ticket to the outside world. It's the rays of sunlight cast through the prison bars. (However, you can't **write** to a web page with **OpenURI**. You'll need to find a tool for copying to your web server. An FTP program, for instance.)

If someone wants to read your diabolical idea about hiding lettuce in the church chairs, assuming you've posted it as a web page:

```
require 'open-uri'

# Opening an idea file available on a web site.
open( "http://your.com/idea-about-hiding-lettuce-in-the-
church-chairs.txt" ) do |idea|
  puts idea.read
end
```

The **OpenURI** library also understands FTP addresses as well. This widens the possibilities for where you can store files. On your system or elsewhere on the Internet.

Reading Files Line by Line

When you're using **OpenURI** to get information from the web with the **open** and **read** methods, the page is given to you as a **String**. You can also read the page one line at a time, if you're searching for something. Or if the page is big and you want to conserve your computer's memory.

```
require 'open-uri'
open( "http://preeventualist.org/lost/
searchfound?q=truck" ) do |truck|
  truck.each_line do |line|
    puts line if line['pickup']
  end
end
```

The above code will retrieve the list of trucks found by preeventualists, then display only those lines that actually contain the word 'pickup'. That way we can trim out the descriptions and look for only the pertinent lines.

Above, the **index brackets** are used on a string, so the string is searched for whatever is inside the brackets. Since the string **'pickup'** is inside the brackets, the **line** string is searched for the word "pickup".

On being funny.

When a web page is loaded with **read**, the entire page is loaded into memory. Usually this only takes up a few thousand bytes. But if a page is big (several megabytes), you'll probably want to use **each_line**, which loads one line at a time to avoid exhausting memory.

Yielding is Kiddie Blocks

Ruby often uses iterators in this fashion. Yes, iterators are used for cycling through each item in a collection of items, such as an array or hash. Now look at an IO source as a collection of lines. The iterator can crawl that collection of lines.

```
class IO
  # Definition for the each_line method.  Notice how it
  # has no argument list.  Blocks don't need to be listed
  # as arguments.
  def each_line
    until eof?      # until we reach the end of the
file...
      yield readline  # pass a line into the block
    end
  end
end
```

The **yield** keyword is the easiest way to use a block. One word. Just like a curtain has a pullstring or like a suitcase has a handle. Inside a method, you can press the blinking **yield** button and it will run the block attached to that method. Glowing a strong red

color until the code inside the block is done. And then it goes back
to blinking and you can press the button again if you like.

```
def yield_thrice
  yield
  yield
  yield
end
```

Punch the **yield** button three times quick and the block gets to
live its life three times.

```
irb> a = ['first, birth.', 'then, a life of flickering
images.', 'and, finally, the end.']
irb> yield_thrice { puts a.shift }
# prints out:
#    first, birth.
#    then, a life of flickering images.
#    and, finally, the end.
```

The **shift** method pulls the first item off an array. The barber
shift cuts the hair off and hands it over. Then, the scalp. And just
keeps going, whittling the poor guy down to nothing.

You've seen blocks attached to methods. Any Ruby method can
have a block attached to the end.

```
# The brief style of attaching a block to a method.
# Here the block is surrounded with curly braces.
open( "idea.txt" ) { |f| f.read }

# The verbose style of attaching a block to a method.
# Here the block is surrounded with `do' and `end'
open( "idea.txt" ) do |f|
  f.read
end
```

If you pass arguments to **yield**, those arguments will also be
passed to the block. The block is riding in a little sidecar attached
to the method's motorcycle. The method yells out a list arguments,

screaming to the block over all the wind as they're racing through the desert. The block taps his helmet like, "I get it, my brain gets it."

```ruby
# The method opens two files and slides the resulting IO
# objects down the chute to an attached block.
def double_open filename1, filename2
  open( filename1 ) do |f1|
    open( filename2 ) do |f2|
      yield f1, f2
    end
  end
end

# Prints the files out side-by-side.
double_open( "idea1.txt", "idea2.txt" ) do |f1, f2|
  puts f1.readline + " | " + f2.readline
end
```

You may also wonder what the **yield** keyword has to do with street signs. And really, it's a good question with, I believe, a good answer. When you run a method, you are giving that method control of your program. Control to do its job and then come back to with an answer.

With **yield**, the method is stopping at the intersection, giving control back to you, to your block. The method is letting you do your work before resuming its work. So while the **each_line** method does the work of actually reading lines from a file, the **block attached to the each_line method** is handed the line itself and gets a chance to hammer away at it in the sidecar.

Preeventualism in a Gilded Box

You've learned so much about **OpenURI** and using **yield** to write your own iterators. You know your way around the lost-and-found service. Really, you can starting hunting through the Wixl junk drawer without me.

Let's neatly *encapsulate* the entire service into a single class.

```ruby
require 'open-uri'
module PreEventualist
  def self.open page, query
    qs =
      query.map do |k, v|
        URI.escape "#{ k }=#{ v }"
      end.join "&"
    URI.parse( "http://preeventualist.org/lost/" + page + "?"
+ qs ).open do |lost|
      lost.read.split( "--\n" )
    end
  end
  def self.search word
    open "search", "q" => word
  end
  def self.searchlost word
    open "searchlost", "q" => word
  end
  def self.searchfound word
    open "searchfound", "q" => word
  end
  def self.addfound your_name, item_lost, found_at, description
    open "addfound", "name" => your_name, "item" => item_lost,
                     "at" => found_at, "desc" => description
  end
  def self.addlost your_name, item_found, last_seen, description
    open "addlost", "name" => your_name, "item" => item_found,
                    "seen" => last_seen, "desc" => description
  end
end
```

At some point with your code, you need to start shaping it into something neat. Save the above module in a file called **preeventualist.rb**.

This module is a very simple library for using the Preeventualist's service. This is exactly the way libraries are written. You whip up a module or a class, store it in a file, and, if you're happy with it and want the world to benefit, put it on the web.

These stragglers can use your module just like I used **OpenURI** earlier.

```
irb> require 'preeventualist'
irb> puts PreEventualist.search( 'truck' )
irb> puts PreEventualist.addfound( 'Why', 'Ruby skills',
'Wixl park', "I can give you Ruby skills!\nCome visit
poignantguide.net!" )
```

2. Meanwhile, The Porcupine Stops To Fill-Up

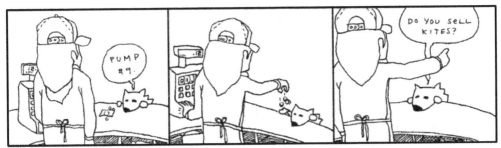

The porcupine pays for gas. Kites?

3. A Sponsored Dragon-Slaying

The slayer hops in.

"Look around," said Fox Small. "Some of us don't have time for quests. Some of us have major responsibilities, jobs, so on. Livelihood, got it?"

"*Heyyyy*, my **JOB** was to kill the drgn!!" screamed the wee rabbit, blinking his eyes and bouncing frantically from tree to tree to pond to pond. "His snout was a **HUGE** responsibility!! His smoky breath was *mine to reckon with!!* I spent fifty dollars on the cab **JUST** to get out there, which was another *huge huge* ordeal. You have *nothing on me*, not a *single* indictment, my whole **HERONESS** is *absoflutely unimpeachable*, my whole **APPROACH** is *abassoonly unapricotable*, just ask Lester."

The Inadvertent Meteor

When I first began my inquiry into preeventualism, I was relayed the following story. I was told that this was all I needed to understand the philosophy.

There was this sculptor who just wasn't satisfied with his work. He had primarily studied traditional subject matter and excelled at sculpting both the human figure and elaborate vegetation. And he was really quite an exquisite sculptor. He just didn't feel like he was making his mark upon the world.

By this time, he had aged well into his fifties and wanted to vaunt into the realm of legendary masters. So he began to construct a massive sculpture of two pears with beads of dew clinging precariously to them.

The sculpture was enormous and hovered ominously above the sculptor's hometown,

held aloof by a massive infrastructure of struts and beams. In fact, the giant pears were so significant that they truly wreaked havoc on the Earth's rotation, ever so slightly, what with a new asteroid-sized fruit basket clinging to it.

The government sent jets and war crafts to destroy the statue. They unleashed a vicious attack on the village, dismantling the statue, blowing it into thousands of pieces, chipping away at it with missiles. Soon enough, the statue was obliterated and all was back to normal.

A huge chunk of the statue had taken orbit in the heavens and often veered perilously close to the planet. When it did, it was always met by an arsenal of advanced weaponry, which further damaged it and deflected its course skyward.

Eventually, this inadvertent meteor was nothing more

than the size of a very daunting man. And, when it at last hit the ground, weathered and polished by its ninety year journey, it was hailed as an enigmatic masterpiece, a message from the great beyond. Here was a stunning likeness of a male nude looking wistfully into the sky with an intricate lace work of vines creeping around his waist and covering his improprieties.

The statue was last sold for fifty-two million dollars and stayed in the permanent exhibit at the Louvre, with the plaque:
"Heavenly Nude"
by Anonymous

"Who's Lester?" said the Fox Small.

"Lester's my cab driver! He parked at the base of Dwemthy's Array!!" The rabbit ricocheted madly like a screensaver for a supercomputer. *"Just ask Dwemthy!!"*

"Well," said the Fox Small. He turned back to look up at Fox Tall, who was sitting straight and looking far into the distance. "Wait, they have a parking lot on Dwemthy's Array?"

"**YEP!!** And a pretzel stand!!"

"But, it's *an Array*? Do they sell churros?"

"**CHOCOLAVA!!**" bleeted the rabbit.

"What about those glow-in-the-dark ropes that you can put in your hair? Or you can just hold them by your side or up in the air—"

"**BRAIDQUEST!!**"

"You should get a cut of the salesman's commission," spoke Fox Small. "Folks came out to see you kill the dragon, right?"

"**BUT!!** I don't operate the tongs that actually extract the chocolava."

"I'm just sayin'. You **do** operate the killing mechanism. So you *have a stake* in the ensalada."

"OH NO!! I left my favorite lettuce leaves in Dwemthy's Array!!" squealed the rabbit, twirling like a celebratory saber through the quaking oak. Distantly: "Or Lester's trunk, maybe?"

"You know—Gheesh, can you stay put??" said Fox Small.

"My radio," said Fox Tall, stirring to life for a moment, "in my pickup." The glaze still seeping from his eyes. His stare quivered and set back into his face, recalling another time and place. A drive out to Maryland. Sounds of Lionel Richie coming in so clearly. The wipers going a bit too fast. He pulls up to a house. His mother answers the door. She is a heavily fluffed fox. Tears and makeup.

Slumping back down, "That porcupine is changing my presets."

The rabbit bounded up on to the armrest of the park bench and spoke closely. "**BUT!!** Soon I will feast on drgn's head and the juices of drgn's tongue!!" The rabbit sat still and held his paws kindly.

"(Which I hope will taste like cinnamon bears,)" whispered the rabbit, intimately.

"I love cinnamon," said Fox Small. "I should go killing with you some time."

"You should," said the rabbit and the eyes shine-shined.

"Although, salivating over a tongue. You don't salivate over it, do you?"

"I DO!!" and the rabbit got so excited that Sticky Whip shot out of his eyes. (More on Sticky Whip in a later sidebar. Don't let me forget. See also: *The Purist's Compendium to Novelty Retinal Cremes* by Jory Patrick Sobgoblin, available wherever animal attachment clips are sold.)

"Okay, you've hooked me. I want to hear all about it," Fox Small declared. "Please, talk freely about the chimbly. Oh, and Dwemthy. Who is he? What makes him tick? Then maybe, if I'm still around after that, you can tell me about what makes rabbits tick, and maybe you can hold our hands through this whole missing truck ordeal. I need consolation more than anything else. I could probably use religion right now. I could use your personal bravery and this sense of accomplishment you exude. Do you smoke a pipe? Could be a handy tool to coax along the pontification we must engage in."

And the rabbit began expounding upon Dwemthy and the legend of Dwemthy and the ways of Dwemthy. As with most stories of Dwemthy, the rabbit's tales were mostly embellishments. Smotchkkiss, there are delicacies which I alone must address.

Please, never ask who Dwemthy is. Obviously he is a mastermind and would never disclose his location or true identity. He has sired dynasties. He has set living ogres aflame. Horses everywhere smell him at all times. Most of all, he knows carnal pleasures. And to think that this...

This is his Array.

Dwemthy's Array

Dwemthy's Array has charmed and tormented the village folk for centuries.

You stand at the entrance of Dwemthy's Array. You are a rabbit who is about to die. And deep at the end of the Array:

```
class Dragon < Creature
  life 1340      # tough scales
  strength 451   # bristling veins
  charisma 1020  # toothy smile
  weapon 939     # fire breath
end
```

A scalding *SEETHING LAVA* infiltrates the **cacauphonous ENGORGED MINESHAFTS** deep within the ageless canopy of the *DWEMTHY FOREST*... chalky and nocturnal screams from **the belly of the RAVENOUS WILD STORKUPINE**... who eats **wet goslings** *RIGHT AFTER* they've had a few graham crackers and a midday nap... amidst starved hippos *TECHNICALLY ORPHANED* but truthfully sheltered by umbrellas owned jointly by car dealership conglomerates... beneath *uncapped vials* of mildly pulpy **BLUE ELIXIR**... *which shall remain... heretofore... UNDISTURBED... DWEMTHY!!!*

Luck and mother nature.

If you don't understand Dwemthy's Array, it is Dwemthy's fault. He designed the game to complicate our lives and were it simpler, it would not be the awe-inspiring quest we've come to cherish in our arms this very hour.

Dwemthy's Array has a winding history of great depth. It is not enough to simply say, "Dwemthy's Array," over and over and expect to build credentials from that act alone. Come with me, I can take you back a couple years, back to the sixties where it all started with metaprogramming and the dolphins.

You might be inclined to think that **metaprogramming** is another hacker word and was first overheard in private phone calls between fax machines. Honest to God, I am here to tell you that it is stranger than that. Metaprogramming began with *taking drugs in the company of dolphins.*

In the sixties, a prolific scientist named John C. Lilly began experimenting with his own senses, to uncover the workings of his body. I can relate to this. I do this frequently when I am standing in the middle of a road holding a pie or when I am hiding inside a cathedral. I pause to examine my self. This has proven to be nigh impossible. I have filled three ruled pages with algebraic notation, none of which has explained anything. The pie, incidentally, has been very easy to express mathematically.

But the scientist Lilly went about his experiments otherwise. He ingested LSD in the company of dolphins. Often in a dark, woeful isolation tank full of warm salt water. Pretty bleak. But it was science! (Lest you think him criminal: until 1966, LSD was supplied by Sandoz Laboratories to any interested scientists, free of charge.)

Drugs, dolphins and deprivation. Which led to Lilly's foray into things meta. He wrote books on mental programming, comparing humans and computers. You may choose to ingest any substance you want during this next quote—most likely you're reaching for the grain of salt—but I assure you that there's no Grateful Dead show on the lawn and no ravers in the basement.

> *When one learns to learn, one is making models, using symbols, analogizing, making metaphors, in short, inventing and using language, mathematics, art, politics, business, etc. At the critical brain (cortex) size, languages and its consequences appear. To avoid the necessity of repeating learning to learn, symbols, metaphors, models each time, I symbolize the underlying idea in these operations as metaprogramming.*

> *John C. Lilly, Programming and Metaprogramming in the Human Biocomputer, New York, 1972.*

We learn. But first we learn to learn. We setup programming in our mind which is the pathway to further programming. (Lilly is largely talking about programming the brain and the nervous system, which he collectively called the *biocomputer.*)

Lilly's metaprogramming was more about feeding yourself imagery, reinventing yourself, all that. This sort of thinking links directly to folks out there who dabble in shamanism, wave their hands over tarot cards and wake up early for karate class. I guess you could say metaprogramming is New Age, but it's all settled down recently into a sleeping bag with plain old nerdiness. (If you got here from a Google search[9] for "C++ Metaprogramming", stick around, but I only ask that you *burn* those neural pathways that originally invoked the search. Many thanks.)

Meta itself is spoken of no differently in your author's present day.

All sensuous response to reality is an interpretation of it. Beetles and monkeys clearly interpret their world, and act on the basis of what they see. Our physical senses are themselves organs of interpretation. What distinguishes us from our fellow animals is that we are able in turn to interpret these interpretations. In that sense, all human language is meta-language. It is a second-order reflection on the 'language' of our bodies—of our sensory apparatus.

Terry Eagleton, After Theory, London, 2003, ch. 3.

To that end, you could say programming itself is a meta-language. *All code* speaks the language of action, of a plan which hasn't been played yet, but shortly will. Stage directions for the players inside your machine. I've waxed sentimental on this before.

But now we're advancing our study, venturing into metaprogramming, but don't sweat it, **it's still just the Ruby you've seen already**, which is why Dwemthy feels no qualms thrusting it at you right away. Soon enough it will be as easy to spot as addition or subtraction. At first it may seem intensely bright, like you've stumbled across your first firefly, which has flown up in your face. Then, it becomes just *a little bobbing light* which makes living in Ohio so much nicer.

---

9 Publisher's note: Google searches are unlikely to have led you directly to this paperback edition.

Bread Riddles

Question: Can one take five bites from a bread and make the shape of a bicycle? Answer: Yes.

Question: Can one rip a bread in half and still fit the bread in an envelope? Answer: Yes.

Question: Can one man take a bread and throw it while another man sits without bread? Answer: Yes.

Question: Can four breads in a box be explained? Answer: Yes.

Question: Can a clerical error in my company books be attributed to bread? Answer: Yes.

Question: Can dancers break through a scrim of bread? Answer: Yes.

Question: Can those same dancers, when faced with an inexplicably different scrim of bread, fail to break through? Answer: Yes.

Question: Does bread understand my darkest fears and wildest dreams? Answer: Yes.

Question: Does bread desire me? Answer: Yes.

Question: Will bread be invisible to robots? Answer: Yes.

Question: Can one robot take eight bites on a bread, without knowing it's there, and make the shape of a smaller bread? Answer: Yes.

Question: Should my clerics be equipped with bread? Answer: Yes.

Question: In relation to bread, will robots each have their own elephants? Answer: Yes.

Question: Can one rip a bread in half and not let it ruin one's game of dominoes? Answer: Yes.

Question: Will we always love bread? Answer: Yes.

Question: Will we have more bread? Answer: Yes.

Question: Can four breads marry a robot's elephant? Answer: Yes.

Metaprogramming is *writing code which writes code*. But not as M.C. Escher would sketch it. **The program isn't reaching back around and overwriting itself, nor is the program jumping onto your screen and wrenching the keyboard from your hands.** No, it's much smaller than that.

Let's say it's more like **a little orange pill** you won at the circus. When you suck on it, the coating wears away and behind your teeth hatches a massive, floppy sponge brontosaurus. He slides down your tongue and leaps free, frolicking over the pastures, yelping, "Papa!" And from then on, whenever he freaks out and attacks a van, well, that van is *sparkling clean* afterwards.

Now, let's say *someone else* puts **their little orange pill** under the faucet. Not on their tongue, *under the faucet*. And this triggers a different catalysm, which births a set of wailing sponge sextuplets. **Umbilical cords and everything.** Still very handy for cleaning the van. But an altogether different kind of chamois. And, one day, these eight will stir Papa to tears when they perform the violin concerto of their lives.

Metaprogramming is packing code into pill-form, such that a slender drop of water could trigger it to expand. More importantly, you can control the pill's reaction, so that a brontosaurus is produced,

scaly and lumbering. Or septulets, **CERTAINLY.** Or seamstresses.
Or cat brains. Or dragons.

```
class Dragon < Creature
  life 1340     # tough scales
  strength 451  # bristling veins
  charisma 1020 # toothy smile
  weapon 939    # fire breath
end
```

This is not metaprogramming yet. Only the pill. The *product*
of metaprogramming. We are pausing, looking at the beast itself
before descending beneath its flesh with a scalpel and microscope.

The **Dragon** is a class. You've seen that many times now. The
Dragon is a descendant of the **Creature** class.

Now, eyes up. Look at me. The **Creature** class contains the
metaprogramming code. You can write metaprogramming code
which can be used *everywhere*, throughout Ruby, in **Creature**
or **Dragon**, in **String** or in **Object**, anywhere. Our example
here, since this is the most common form of meta-code, focuses on
metaprogramming inside your own classes only.

Each of the **Dragon**'s traits are simply **class methods**. You
could also write this as:

```
class Dragon < Creature
  life( 1340 )     # tough scales
  strength( 451 )  # bristling veins
  charisma( 1020 ) # toothy smile
  weapon( 939 )    # fire breath
end
```

Removing the parens removes clutter, so let's leave them out.
Only use parens when you are using several methods together and
you want to be very clear.

Creature Code

Now, with a lateral slice across the diaphragm, we expose
the innards of **Creature**. **Save this code into a file
called dwemthy.rb.**

```ruby
# The guts of life force within Dwemthy's Array
class Creature

  # Get a metaclass for this class
  def self.metaclass; class << self; self; end; end

  # Advanced metaprogramming code for nice, clean traits
  def self.traits( *arr )
    return @traits if arr.empty?

    # 1. Set up accessors for each variable
    attr_accessor( *arr )

    # 2. Add a new class method to for each trait.
    arr.each do |a|
      metaclass.instance_eval do
        define_method( a ) do |val|
          @traits ||= {}
          @traits[a] = val
        end
      end
    end

    # 3. For each monster, the `initialize' method
    #     should use the default number for each trait.
    class_eval do
      define_method( :initialize ) do
        self.class.traits.each do |k,v|
          instance_variable_set("@#{k}", v)
        end
      end
    end

  end

  # Creature attributes are read-only
  traits :life, :strength, :charisma, :weapon
end
```

Focus on the closing lines of code, specifically the line where the **traits** are being set up. All of the code before that line sets up the **traits** class method. This bears resemblance to the basic lottery tickets from the chapter previous.

```
class LotteryTicket
  attr_reader :picks, :purchased
end
```

Both **traits** and **attr_reader** are simply class methods. When **attr_reader** is used in the **LotteryTicket**, metaprogramming kicks in behind the scenes and starts blowing up balloons, creating **reader** methods for the instance variables **@picks** and **@purchased** above.

The code for the **traits** method is the metaprogramming I've been alluding to. Comments in the code reveal the three stages the method goes through when adding traits.

1. The **list of traits is passed on to attr_accessor**, which builds **reader** and **writer** code for instance variables. One for each trait.

2. **Class methods are added** for each trait. (A **life** class method is added for a **:life** trait.) These class methods are used in the class definition just like you would use **traits** or **attr_accessor**. This way, you can specify the trait, along with the points given for a trait to a certain creature.

3. **Add an initialize method** which sets up a new monster properly, grabbing the right points and *POWER UP! POWER UP!* the monster is alive!

The beauty of these three steps is that you've taught Ruby how to code monsters for you. So when Ruby gets to the **traits**:

```
class Creature
  traits :life, :strength, :charisma, :weapon
end
```

Ruby fills in the code behind the scenes and transplants a spiny green heart and jumpstarts the body with a pullcord. Ruby will use the metaprogramming from the **Creature** class and build out all the various methods, expanding the **traits** list like this:

```ruby
class Creature

  # 1. set up reader and writer methods
  attr_accessor :life, :strength, :charisma, :weapon

  # 2. add new class methods to use in creature
  def self.life( val )
    @traits ||= {}
    @traits['life'] = val
  end

  def self.strength( val )
    @traits ||= {}
    @traits['strength'] = val
  end

  def self.charisma( val )
    @traits ||= {}
    @traits['charisma'] = val
  end

  def self.weapon( val )
    @traits ||= {}
    @traits['weapon'] = val
  end

  # 3. initialize sets the default points for
  #     each trait
  def initialize
    self.class.traits.each do |k,v|
      instance_variable_set("@#{k}", v)
    end
  end

end
```

Now, Ruby will gladly accept this six-line **Dragon** code, short enough to look nice when printed on playing cards:

```ruby
class Dragon < Creature
  life 1340      # tough scales
  strength 451   # bristling veins
  charisma 1020  # toothy smile
  weapon 939      # fire breath
end
```

Eval, the Littlest Metaprogrammer

While the metaprogramming code above is just plain Ruby, it can be difficult to follow still. I totally understand if you've come to this point and your eyes are spinning in their sockets and your knees have locked up. The trickiest parts of the above are the lines which call the methods **instance_eval** and **class_eval**. Just rub some tiger balm on your joints while I talk about **eval**.

We've been talking about **metaprogramming**. Writing code which writes code. The **eval** method hangs out in this alley. The vagrant **eval** takes code you have stored up in a string and it executes that code.

```ruby
drgn = Dragon.new
# is identical to...
drgn = eval( "Dragon.new" )
# or, alternatively...
eval( "drgn = Dragon.new" )
```

Here, let's write a program which has a hole in it. Instead of writing a program which creates a new **Dragon**, let's leave a hole where the **Dragon** would be.

```ruby
print "What monster class have you come to battle? "
monster_class = gets
eval( "monster = " + monster_class + ".new" )
p monster
```

The program asks for a monster. If you type in **Dragon**, then the **monster_class** variable will contain the string **"Dragon"**.

Inside the **eval**, a few strings get added together to make the string **"monster = Dragon.new"**. And when the **eval** executes this string, the **monster** variable contains a **Dragon** object. Ready for battle.

This is great! Now we can leave it up to the player to pick a monster! Of course, we're trusting the player to supply a real monster class. If they type in **BotanicalWitch** and there is no **BotanicalWitch** class, they'll get an exception tossed in their face.

So, in short, **eval** lets you make up code as you go. Which can be useful and which can be dangerous as well.

The **instance_eval** and **class_eval** method used in the metaprogramming for the **Creature** class are slightly different from the normal **eval**. These two special methods run code just like **eval** does, but they duck into classes and objects and run the code there.

```
# The instance_eval method runs code as if it were run
# inside an object's instance method.
irb> drgn = Dragon.new
irb> drgn.instance_eval do
irb>   @name = "Tobias"
irb> end

irb> drgn.instance_variable_get( "@name" )
  => "Tobias"

# The class_eval method runs code is if inside a class
# definition.
irb> Dragon.class_eval do
irb>   def name; @name; end
irb> end

irb> drgn.name
  => "Tobias"
```

As you can see above, the **instance_eval** and **class_eval** methods also can take a code block instead of a string. Which is just how things are done in Dwemthy's Array.

Enough Belittling Instruction and Sly Juxtaposition—Where Is Dwemthy's Array??

Tread carefully—here is **the other half of DWEMTHY'S ARRAY!!**
Add these lines to `dwemthy.rb`.

```ruby
class Creature
  # This method applies a hit taken during a fight.
  def hit( damage )
    p_up = rand( charisma )
    if p_up % 9 == 7
      @life += p_up / 4
      puts "[#{ self.class } magick powers up #{ p_up }!]"
    end
    @life -= damage
    puts "[#{ self.class } has died.]" if @life <= 0
  end

  # This method takes one turn in a fight.
  def fight( enemy, weapon )
    if life <= 0
      puts "[#{ self.class } is too dead to fight!]"
      return
    end

    # Attack the opponent
    your_hit = rand( strength + weapon )
    puts "[You hit with #{ your_hit } points of damage!]"
    enemy.hit( your_hit )

    # Retaliation
    p enemy
    if enemy.life > 0
      enemy_hit = rand( enemy.strength + enemy.weapon )
      puts "[Your enemy hit with #{ enemy_hit } points of
damage!]"
      self.hit( enemy_hit )
    end
  end
end
```

```ruby
class DwemthysArray < Array
  alias _inspect inspect
  def inspect; "#<#{ self.class }#{ _inspect }>"; end
  def method_missing( meth, *args )
    answer = first.send( meth, *args )
    if first.life <= 0
      shift
      if empty?
        puts "[Whoa. You decimated Dwemthy's Array!]"
      else
        puts "[Get ready. #{ first.class } has emerged.]"
      end
    end
    answer || 0
  end
end
```

This code adds two methods to **Creature**. The **hit** method which reacts to a hit from another **Creature**. And the **fight** method which lets you place your own blows against that **Creature**.

When your **Creature** takes a hit, a bit of defense kicks in and your **charisma** value is used to generate a power-up. Don't ask me to explain the secrets behind this phenomenon. A random number is picked, some simple math is done, and, if you're lucky, you get a couple life points. **@life += p_up / 4**.

Then, the enemy's blow is landed. **@life -= damage**. That's how the **Creature#hit** method works.

The **fight** method checks to see if your **Creature** is alive. Next, a random hit is placed on your opponent. If your opponent lives through the hit, it gets a chance to strike back. Those are the workings of the **Creature#fight** method.

I'll explain **DwemthysArray** in a second. I really will. I'm having fun doing it. Let's stick with hitting and fighting for now.

Introducing: You.

You may certainly tinker with derivations on this rabbit. But official Dwemthy Paradigms explicitly denote the code—and the altogether character—inscribed below. **Save this as rabbit.rb**.

```ruby
class Rabbit < Creature
  traits :bombs

  life 10
  strength 2
  charisma 44
  weapon 4
  bombs 3

  # little boomerang
  def ^( enemy )
    fight( enemy, 13 )
  end
  # the hero's sword is unlimited!!
  def /( enemy )
    fight( enemy, rand( 4 + ( ( enemy.life % 10 ) ** 2 ) ) )
  end
  # lettuce will build your strength and extra ruffage
  # will fly in the face of your opponent!!
  def %( enemy )
    lettuce = rand( charisma )
    puts "[Healthy lettuce gives you #{ lettuce } life points!!]"
    @life += lettuce
    fight( enemy, 0 )
  end
  # bombs, but you only have three!!
  def *( enemy )
    if @bombs.zero?
      puts "[UHN!! You're out of bombs!!]"
      return
    end
    @bombs -= 1
    fight( enemy, 86 )
  end
end
```

You have four weapons. The boomerang. The hero's sword. The lettuce. And the bombs.

To start off, open up **irb** and load the libraries we've created above.

```
irb> require 'dwemthy'
irb> require 'rabbit'
```

Now, unroll yourself.

```
irb> r = Rabbit.new
irb> r.life
  => 10
irb> r.strength
  => 2
```

Good, good.

Rabbit Fights ScubaArgentine!

You cannot just go rushing into Dwemthy's Array, unseatbelted and merely perfumed!! You must advance deliberately through the demonic cotillion. Or south, through the thickets and labyrinth of coal.

For now, let's lurk covertly through the milky residue alongside the aqueducts. And sneak up on the **ScubaArgentine**.

```
class ScubaArgentine < Creature
  life 46
  strength 35
  charisma 91
  weapon 2
end
```

To get the fight started, make sure you've created one of you and one of the **ScubaArgentine**.

```
irb> r = Rabbit.new
irb> s = ScubaArgentine.new
```

Now use the little boomerang!

```
irb> r ^ s
[You hit with 2 points of damage!]
#<ScubaArgentine:0x808c864 @charisma=91, @strength=35, @life=44,
@weapon=2>
[Your enemy hit with 28 points of damage!]
[Rabbit has died.]
```

For crying out loud!! Our sample rabbit died!!

The Shoes Which Lies Are Made Of

Earlier, I told you that "The Inadvertant Meteor" was the only story you need to know in order to understand preeventualism. But, really, all you need to understand about preeventualism is that it is still in its infancy and any of its most basic concepts could change.

Which is why I've authored a competing story which I believe uncovers an entirely different and very relevant intellectual scenario.

There was a guy who had been around the block. And he wasn't very old, so he decided to write a biography of his life.

Well, he started to lie in his biography. He made up some stories. But mostly little stories that were inconsequential. Filler. Like he had a story about a painting he'd done of a red background with elephant legs in front.

But he hadn't ever painted anything of the sort. He further embellished the story by talking about a pricey auction he'd snuck into. An auction in New York City where he'd he overheard his painting go to sale for twenty grand. But that wasn't the point of the story. The point was that he could fold his body to fit under a lid on a banquet tray. People would raise the lid and they wouldn't even notice him bracing himself inside. He didn't even mention the price his painting sold at.

Anyway, he really started to like that story (and others like it), to the point where he started to ignore his friends and family, instead preferring to watch what his lie self did after the auction. In his head.

So, then, one day he was shopping and he found a pair of shoes that had stripey laces. And he grabbed the shoes and went to the store counter, forcing them in the cashier's face, yelling, "Look! Look at these! Look! These are the shoes my lie self would wear!" And he bought the shoes and put them on and the whole Earth cracked open and the cash register popped open and swallowed him up and he was suddenly elsewhere, in his lie apartment, sitting down to paint dolphin noses, three of them on a green background.

It was a lot of work, painting all those noses. And he went broke for a while and had to stoop so low as to filming abominable snowman NASCAR.

Grim prospects. I can't ask you to return to the rabbit kingdom, though. Just pretend like you didn't die and make a whole new rabbit.

```
irb> r = Rabbit.new

# attacking with boomerang!
irb> r ^ s

# the hero's sword slashes!
irb> r / s

# eating lettuce gives you life!
irb> r % s

# you have three bombs!
irb> r * s
```

Pretty neat looking, wouldn't you say? The code in **rabbit.rb** alters a few math symbols which work only with the **Rabbit**. Ruby allows you to change the behavior of math operators. After all, **math operators are just methods!**

```
# the boomerang is normally an XOR operator.
irb> 1.^( 1 )
   => 0

# the hero's sword normally divides numbers.
irb> 10./( 2 )
   => 5

# the lettuce gives the remainder of a division.
irb> 10.%( 3 )
   => 1

# the bomb is for multiplication.
irb> 10.*( 3 )
   => 30
```

Where it makes sense, you may choose to use math operators on some of your Classes. Ruby uses these math operators on many of its own classes. Arrays, for example, have a handful of math operators which you can see in the list of instance methods when you type: **ri Array**.

```
# the plus operator combines two arrays into a
single array
irb> ["D", "W", "E"] + ["M", "T", "H", "Y"]
  => ["D", "W", "E", "M", "T", "H", "Y"]

# minus removes all items in the second array found in
the first
irb> ["D", "W", "E", "M", "T", "H", "Y"] - ["W", "T"]
  => ["D", "E", "M", "H", "Y"]

# the multiplier repeats the elements of an array
irb> ["D", "W"] * 3
  => ["D", "W", "D", "W", "D", "W"]
```

You may be wondering: what does this mean for math, though? What if I add the number three to an array? What if I add a string and a number? **How is Ruby going to react?**

Please remember these operators are just methods. But, since these operators *aren't readable words*, it can be harder to tell what they do. Use **ri**. Often you'll find that the operators are identical to other readable methods. You can then choose to use the operator or the method. Whichever is clearer to you.

```
# divide with an operator method ...
irb> 10 / 3
  => 3

# ... or a readable method?
irb> 10.div 3
  => 3
```

And that's how the Rabbit's sword divides.

The Harsh Realities of Dwemthy's Array AWAIT YOU TO MASH YOU!!

Once you're done playchoking the last guy with his oxygen tube, it's time to enter The Array. I doubt you can do it. You left your hatchet at home. And I hope you didn't use all your bombs on the easy guy.

You have six foes.

```
class IndustrialRaverMonkey < Creature
  life 46
  strength 35
  charisma 91
  weapon 2
end

class DwarvenAngel < Creature
  life 540
  strength 6
  charisma 144
  weapon 50
end

class AssistantViceTentacleAndOmbudsman < Creature
  life 320
  strength 6
  charisma 144
  weapon 50
end

class TeethDeer < Creature
  life 655
  strength 192
  charisma 19
  weapon 109
end
```

```
class IntrepidDecomposedCyclist < Creature
  life 901
  strength 560
  charisma 422
  weapon 105
end

class Dragon < Creature
  life 1340    # tough scales
  strength 451    # bristling veins
  charisma 1020 # toothy smile
  weapon 939    # fire breath
end
```

These are the living, breathing monstrosities of Dwemthy's Array. I don't know how they got there. No one knows. Actually, I'm guessing the **IntrepidDecomposedCyclist** rode his ten-speed. But the others: NO ONE knows.

If it's really important for you to know, let's just say the others were born there. Can we move on??

As Dwemthy's Array gets deeper, the challenge becomes more difficult.

```
dwary = DwemthysArray[IndustrialRaverMonkey.new,
                      DwarvenAngel.new,
                      AssistantViceTentacleAndOmbudsman.new,
                      TeethDeer.new,
                      IntrepidDecomposedCyclist.new,
                      Dragon.new]
```

Fight the Array and the monsters will appear as you go. Godspeed and may you return with harrowing tales and nary an angel talon piercing through your shoulder.

Start here:

```
| irb> r % dwary
```

Oh, and none of this "I'm too young to die" business. I'm sick of that crap. I'm not going to have you insulting our undead young people. They are our future. After our future is over, that is.

The rabbit has changed us.

The Making of Dwemthy's Array

Fast forward to a time when the winds have calmed. The dragon is vanquished. The unwashed masses bow. We love you. We are loyal to you.

But what is this centipede nibbling in your eardrum? You dig with your finger, but you can't get him out! Blasted! It's that infernal Dwemthy's Array again. **Explain yourself Dwemthy!**

Here, I shall unmask the Array itself for you.

```ruby
class DwemthysArray < Array
  alias _inspect inspect
  def inspect; "#<#{ self.class }#{ inspect }>"; end
  def method_missing( meth, *args )
    answer = first.send( meth, *args )
    if first.life <= 0
      shift
      if empty?
        puts "[Whoa.  You decimated Dwemthy's Array!]"
      else
        puts "[Get ready. #{ first.class } has emerged.]"
      end
    end
    answer || 0
  end
end
```

By now, you're probably feeling very familiar with inheritance. The **DwemthysArray** class inherits from **Array** and, thus, behaves just like one. For being such a mystery, it's alarmingly brief, yeah?

So it's an Array. Filled with monsters. But what does this extra code do?

Inspect

The **inspect** method isn't really a necessary part of Dwemthy's Array. It's something Dwemthy added as a courtesy to his guests. (Many call him twisted, many call him austere, but we'd all be ignorant to go without admiring the footwork he puts in for us.)

Every object in Ruby has an **inspect** method. It is defined in the **Object** class, so it trickles down through the pedigree to every wee child object just born.

```
irb> o = Object.new
  => #<Object:0x81d60c0>
irb> o.inspect
  => "#<Object:0x81d60c0>"
```

Have you noticed this? Whenever we create an object in **irb**, this noisy **#<Object>** verbage stumbles out! It's a little name badge for the object. The **inspect** method creates that name badge. The badge is just a string.

```
irb> class Rabbit
irb>   attr_accessor :slogan
irb>   def initialize s; @slogan = s; end
irb>   def inspect; "#<#{ self.class } says '#{ @slogan
}'>"; end
irb> end

irb> class FakeRabbit < Rabbit
irb> end

irb> Rabbit.new "i blow'd the drgn's face off!!"
  => #<Rabbit says 'i blow'd the drgn's face off!!'>
irb> FakeRabbit.new "Thusly and thusly and thusly..."
  => #<FakeRabbit says 'Thusly and thusly and thusly...'>
```

The thing is: **irb** is talking back. Every time you run some code in **irb**, the *return value* from that code is inspected. How handy. It's a little conversation between you and **irb**. And **irb** is just reiterating what you're saying so you can see it for your self.

You could write your own Ruby prompt very easily:

```
loop do
  print ">> "
  puts  "=> " + eval( gets ).inspect
end
```

This prompt won't let you write Ruby code longer than a single line. It's the essence of interactive Ruby, though. How do you like that? Two of your recently learned concepts have come together in a most flavorful way. The **eval** takes the typed code and runs it. The response from **eval** is then inspected.

Now, as you are fighting monsters in **irb**, Dwemthy's Array will be inspected and reply with the monsters you have left to fight.

The foxes eat out.

Method Missing

Don't you hate it when you yell "Deirdre!" and like ten people answer? That *never* happens in Ruby. If you call the **deirdre** method, only one **deirdre** method answers. You can't have two methods named the same. If you add a second **deirdre** method, the first one disappears.

You can, however, have a method which **answers to many names**.

```
class NameCaller
  def method_missing( name, *args )
    puts "You're calling `#{name}' and you say:"
    args.each { |say| puts "   " + say }
    puts "But no one is there yet."
  end
  def deirdre( *args )
    puts "Deirdre is right here and you say:"
    args.each { |say| puts "   " + say }
    puts "And she loves every second of it."
    puts "(I think she thinks you're poetic.)"
  end
end
```

When you call the method **deirdre** above, I'm sure you know what will happen. Deirdre will love every second of it, you and your dazzling poetry.

But what if you call **simon**?

```
irb> NameCaller.new.simon( 'Hello?', 'Hello? Simon?' )
You're calling `simon' and you say:
  Hello?
  Hello? Simon?
But no one is there yet.
```

Yes, **method_missing** is like an answering machine, which intercepts your method call. In Dwemthy's Array we use call forwarding, so that when you attack the Array, it passes that attack on straight to the first monster in the Array.

```
def method_missing( meth, *args )
  answer = first.send( meth, *args )
  # ... snipped code here ...
end
```

See! See! That skinny little **method_missing** passes the buck!

4. So, Let's Be Clear: The Porcupine Is Now To The Sea

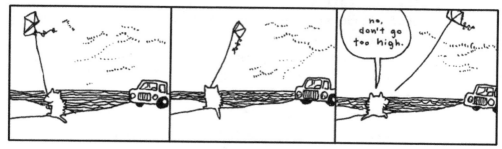

The porcupine and his kite.

5. Walking, Walking, Walking, Walking and So Forth

The evening grew dark around the pair of foxes. They had wound their way through alleys packed with singing possums, and streets where giraffes in rumpled sportscoats bumped past them with their briefcases. They kept walking.

And now the stores rolled shut their corrugated metal lids. Crickets crawled out from the gutters and nudged at the loose change.

Why such hard feelings?

"Anyway, you must admit he's a terrible President," said Fox Small. *"Why* does President Marcos have a rabbit as Vice President of the Foxes."

"The Vice President? The rabbit with the *eyebrows*?"

"No, the rabbit with the **huge sausage lips**," said Fox Small.

But their conversation was abruptly interrupted by a freckly cat head which popped from the sky just above the sidewalk.

At least they're still in the book...

What is this about?!

Will the book finish?

Oh, come on. This is rich. More meta.

I'm not going to bother illustrating this discussion Blixy had with the foxes at this point! It's all a **bunch of *conjecture*.** *HOW* can they presume to know the landscape of my family drama? I love my sister. For a long time, I *worshipped* her. (This is my sister Quil.)

I admit that there was a pretty painful day a few months ago and I kind of freaked out. I was laid out on the long patio chair by the pool in my mom's backyard. I had a Dr. Pepper and a bit of German chocolate cake. I was eating with a kid fork. Everything else was in the dishwasher, that's all they had. Three prongs.

My mom started talking about Quil. All about how much money she was blowing on pants and purses. A five-hundred dollar purse. And then she said, "She's losing it. She sounded totally high on the phone." (She nailed it on the head, Quil was smoking dope and loving it.)

So I'd been noticing how observant my mom could be. That's why, when she said, "I actually think she's on cocaine," I *physically* stood up and chucked my soda across the yard.

It sailed off into the woods somewhere. We had been talking awhile, so it was dark when the can flew. I paced a bit. And then I screamed at the top of my lungs.

My uncle Mike was standing there with the glass door open, staring at me. He said something totally nervous like, "Oh, okay. Well, I'll—" And the tea in his glass was swishing back and forth, sloshing all over. He disappeared. He's not very good at saying things to people. He's more of a whistler. And resonant.

Moving along.

So, to be completely honest, yes, I got a little mad. I got mad. You know. I dealt with it. Quil calls me regularly. For some stupid reason, I rarely call her.

Plus, she didn't end up killing herself. So it's just not an issue. Who knows if it was real. She just had a lot of vodka. And she's little. So it was just scary to see Quil guzzling it down like that. I mean forcing it down.

But why talk about it? It'll just make her feel like I'm disappointed. Or like I'm a jerk.

Well, I got off track there a bit. Where was I? Blix is basically helping the foxes around, getting them on the trail of their truck. Yeah, back to all that.

Frogs who save seats on the bus.

"We can't squeeze on to this bus," said the smallest fox.

"Guys, walk on up," said Blix. "What's the hold up? Oh, the frogs. Yeah, just squeeze through." Blixy pushed from behind.

"Hey," said the Tall Fox. "I'm crammed on this little step! Somebody move!"

"Did you get through—young fox??" said the cat.

"No," said Fox Small, "can't you see? The driver keeps shaking his head and it's *really* making me nervous. I don't think he wants us on."

"Go," said Blix. He stepped down from his step and walked around the bus, peering through the plexiglass windows. "Well, I don't know, guys. I dunno. I guess it's got a lot of frogs." He pounded on the window. "Hey! Move over!"

And that's the reality of riding intercity transit in Wixl. It's terribly competitive. The morning bus is so crowded that most white collar animals get frogs to hold their seat through the nighttime. For whatever reason, it works. It's become this staple of their workflow and their economy.

If you can muster up a bit of imagination, you can see a **percent sign** as a frog's slanted face. Got the picture in your head? Now let me show you frogs that camp out inside strings.

```
# The %s format is for placing full strings.
irb> "Seats are taken by %s and %s." % ['a frog', 'a frog
with teeth']
  => "Seats are taken by a frog and a frog with teeth."


# The %d format is for placing numbers, while the %f
# format is for floats (decimal numbers).
irb> frogs = [44, 162.30]
irb> stats = "Frogs have filled %d seats and paid %f blue
crystals."
irb> stats % frogs
  => "Frogs have filled 44 seats and paid 162.30 blue
crystals."


# Formatting is flexible with types, you can pass in
# strings and format them like numbers.
irb> frogs = ['44', '162.30']
irb> stats % frogs
  => "Frogs have filled 44 seats and paid 162.30 blue
crystals."
```

What you are seeing above uses the **%** method in the **String** class. This method takes **a string** and **an array** and slurps them in together to create a new string. The items from the list are yanked out (in order) and placed in their saved seats. It's the open of the business day and the frogs have done their job.

```
# See, here's the String#% method called like other
methods.
irb> "Please move over, %s.".%( 'toothless frog' )
  => "Please move over, toothless frog"


# Now let's call it the prettier way, with the percent
sign
# right between the string and the array.
irb> "Here is your 1098 statement for the year, %s." %
['teeth frog']
  => "Here is your 1098 statement for the year, teeth
frog."
```

This is also available as the **Kernel::format** method or **Kernel::sprintf** method. (In the C language, there is a **sprintf** method which operates just like this.)

```
irb> format "Frogs are piled %d deep and travel at %d
mph.", [5, 56]
  => "Frogs are piled 5 deep and travel at 56 mph."
```

For the most part, you'll only need **%s** (strings), **%d** (integer numbers) or **%f** (float numbers) format specifiers. The **%p** placeholder will run **inspect** on an object.

Yeah, so, frog formatting is really handy for building strings that are assembled from different kinds of data. You can learn all the various kinds of format specifiers by reading the **ri sprintf** page. I'm just going to give you a few quick pointers.

Let's say you have the array but you want the items to appear in **a different order** in the string. In such a situation, you can identify specific items by placing a number (**1$** for the first item, **2$** for the second, and so on) right after the percent sign.

```
irb> "This bus has %1$d more stops before %2$d o'clock.
That's %1$d more stops." % [16, 8]
  => "This bus has 16 more stops before 8 o'clock.
That's 16 more stops."
```

The second tip I have for you is that you can allot a certain number of characters for each item, a width. And if an item is smaller than the width, extra spaces will be used before the item, to pad it. If the width is a negative number, the item will be forced to left and the padding will come after it.

```
# Give one item 30 characters of width
irb> "In the back of the bus: %30s." % ['frogs']
  => "In the back of the bus:                          frogs."

# Give one left-justified item 30 characters of width
irb> "At the front of the bus: %-30s." % ['frogs']
  => "At the front of the bus: frogs                          ."
```

Fox Small kept looking up at the bus driver. Remember, he wouldn't enter the bus!

"What's the deal?" said Fox Tall. "Can't you just get on and we'll just stand in the aisle?"

"You really want to get on this bus? That driver has no hands," said Fox Small, speaking close and hushed to Fox Tall, "and all he has, instead of hands, are sucker cups."

More From The Chilling Ongoing Preview of The Scarf Eaters

(from Chapter XII: Thank Heaven for Little Men.)

"Close the door," Spencer repeated, but Lara's hand trembled and she fumbled sloppily at the latch. Her dad hadn't taught her to close doors like this one.

"Yes, it's an unusual door," said Brent. He walked over and closed the door for her. Then, he held her hand and looked into her eyes. His eyes lit up like huge matchsticks that would be too huge to be practical. "It's an unusual handle, which ensures that those who don't eat scarves stay out."

"Sit down, everyone," Spencer demanded, as he bounded across the room and took command. "I command this organization," he stated. "The secret organization of The Scarf Eaters!"

The torches encircling the room blazed like invincibly huge matches and the handful of teenagers sat. Except for Spencer who stood high and mighty, drawing all the oxygen in the entire room into his nostrils before speaking.

"One of us," he said, dramatically and invincibly, "is missing!"

The entire room gasped, which also used oxygen. The room was abuzz. "Who?" "How?" "Who was it?" Nobody knew. Except for Spencer, who leapt across the room and took charge.

"Our dear friend Steve Bridell has been stolen from us," announced Spencer in a deafeningly loud voice, as if thousands of giant matchsticks were struck against a brittle surface in unison amidst a pile of oxygen. "Steve Bridell. Do any of you know Steve Bridell?"

The hall was silent.

Spencer continued. "Steve Bridell was an incredible resource and you all knew him and loved him. He carved this enormous wooden man we use as our podium." Spencer pointed. "He also made the set of wooden cymbals that are back in our instrument closet right now."

Some of the audience stood.

"Wait," instructed Spencer. "Don't go back there. I've already checked. The cymbals are gone!"

"So what? You don't think animals with tentacles can drive?"

"Well, not only is he going to flub up the steering wheel but he has all these legs all over the foot pedals. This is not smart. Let's get another bus. Come on."

"You know, he's probably been driving like that all day. Is he really going to start crashing at this point in his career?"

"Buses do crash," said Fox Small. "Some do. This smells crashworthy."

"Sheer doo-doo!" And Fox Tall yelled to the driver, "Hey, cabby, how long have you been driving this bus for?"

The bus driver peered over darkly under his cap and started to turn toward them, but his tentacles were stuck to the wheel. He jerked swiftly at his forelegs and, failing their release, he turned to the wheel and focused his energies on milking his glands for some slicker secretions. Bubbles of mucus oozed.

"Let's get outta here," said Fox Tall and the two ran off into the street, slamming right into the cat Blix.

"Alright, well, the bus is full," said Blix. "I don't know why the driver stopped if he knew the bus was crammed with hoppers."

"We're thinking he was about to crash into us," said Fox Tall, "and he opened the door to make it look like a planned route stop."

"Keep in mind, Blix, we hadn't really discussed that possibility out loud, so I haven't had a chance to formally agree," said Fox Small. "Nevertheless, it sounds rational to me."

"I'm thinking all the buses are going to be full like this." Blix bit his lip, thinking and flicking his eyes about. "Let's just—" He pointed down the circuitry of apartment buildings that wound to the south. "But maybe—" He looked up and surveyed the stars, scratching his head and counting the constellations with very small poking motions from the tip of his finger.

"Are you getting our bearings from the stars and planets?" asked Fox Small.

Blix didn't speak, he ducked off to the north through a poorly laid avenue back behind the paint store. But before we follow them down that service road, Smotchkkiss, I have one more frog for you, perched on a long lilypad that stretches out to hold anything at all.

```
irb> cat = "Blix"
irb> puts "Does #{ cat } see what's up?  Is #{ cat }
aware??"
   => "Does Blix see what's up?  Is Blix aware??"
```

The little frogs from earlier (**%s** or **%d**) were only placeholders for single strings. Saving places in the string.

The lilypads above start with a flower bud, the **octothorpe**. You've also seen it as a pound sign on telephones. After the flower bud, two leaves form the edges of the lilypad. The leaves are **curly braces**, also seen many times before as the *crab pincers* for a code block.

An empty lilypad **"#{}"** becomes an empty string **""**.

When the lilypad is found in a **double-quoted** string, Ruby runs any code found in between the two leaves of the lilypad. The lilypad is lifted out and the result of the code is placed there in the string. This lilypad swap is called *string interpolation*.

```
irb> fellows = ['Blix', 'Fox Tall', 'Fox Small']
irb> puts "Let us follow #{ fellows.join ' and ' } on their
journey."
  => "Let us follow Blix and Fox Tall and Fox Small on their
journey."
```

The lilypad is very durable and can hold any kind of code inside. Above we are using **Array#join**, but you can do anything you like inside. Call object methods, conditional **if** or **case** statements, even define classes.

```
irb> blix_went = :north
irb> puts "Blix didn't speak, he ducked off to the #{ blix_
went } through #{
                if blix_went == :north
                  'a poorly laid avenue behind the paint store'
                elsif blix_went == :south
                  'the circuitry of apartment buildings'
                else
                  '... well, who knows where he went.'
                end }.  But before we follow them..."
=> "Blix didn't speak, he ducked off to the north through a
poorly laid avenue behind the paint store.  But before we
follow them..."
```

The foxes followed Blixy off behind the paint store and down the cracked, uneven asphalt. All of the stores on the dilapidated lane leaned at angles to each other. In some places, slabs of sidewalk jutted up from the ground, forming a perilous walkway, a disorderly stack of ledges. Almost as if the city planners had hoped to pay tribute to the tectonic plates. One small drug store had slid below the surface, nearly out of eyesight.

Truly, it was colorful, though. The paint store had been tossing out old paints directly onto its neighbors. The shops nearest the paint store were clogged with hundreds of colors, along the windowsills and in the rain gutters. Yes, on the walls and pavement.

Basically, beginning with the back porch of the paint store, the avenue erupted into a giant incongruous and poorly-dyed market.

Further down, a dentist's office was primed with red paint and, over that, a fledgling artist had depicted a large baby who had fallen through a chimney and arrived in a fireplace full of soot. Crude black strokes marked the cloud of ashes raised during impact, easily mistaken for thick hair on the child's arms and back. The child looked far too young to have much hair, but there they were: rich, blonde curls which toppled liberally from the child's head. Under the child's legs was painted the word *BREWSTER*.

The same artist had hit the library next store and had hastily slapped together a mural of a green sports car being pulled from the mud by a team of legless babies tugging with shiny chains. Again, the drastically blonde curls!

"I need answers," said the Fox Tall, who had ground to a halt in front of the scenery.

"I'm starting to believe there's no such thing," said Fox Small. "Maybe these are the answers."

"Brewster?" said Fox Tall. He walked nearer to the library and touched the cheek of one of the legless children who was closer in perspective. The child's cheek appeared to contain a myriad of jawbones.

Blix was another two houses down, navigating through the askew brickwork, the paved gully that led to *R.K.'s Gorilla Mint*, as the metallic sticker on the door read. The building was plastered with miniature logos for the variety of payment options and identification acceptable at *R.K.'s Gorilla Mint*. Even the bars over the window were lined with insurance disclosures and security warnings and seals of government authorization, as well as addendums to all of these, carbon paper covering stickers covering torn posters and advertising. And all mingled with paint splashes that intruded wherever they pleased.

R.K.'s Gorilla Mint.

"I like the way the fresh paper feels against my tongue," said the gorilla at the counter. His fingers rubbed quietly against the bills. He drew his face near to the fanned currency and whisked his nose along the pulpy cash.

"Is R.K. in this evening?" asked Blix.

"R.K. is not," said the gorilla cashier. He turned to the three travelers and spread his money out on the counter's surface, evenly spacing them apart and lining up all the edges neatly. "Now, which one of these do you think is worth the most?"

The foxes looked over the different bills and Fox Small muttered to himself, "Well, maybe—no, but I'll bet—Wait, does one of these have bananas on it? 'Cause that one—nope, no fruit or rope swings or—Terrible, this is difficult!" And in a lower voice, "So difficult to read. What does this one say? Symbols or something? If all these bills have are symbols, it's going to be impossible for us to figure out which one is of the greatest value."

"That's why I said, '*Guess.*'" The gorilla tapped each bill in order. "See, you've got a 1 in 5 chance."

"Unless the symbols mean something," said Fox Tall. "Unless we can figure it out."

"We can figure it out," said Fox Small.

"No," said the gorilla. "The symbols are meaningless."

"Whoever created the money intended some meaning for them," said Fox Small. "Why use *this* symbol?" He pointed to an ampersand printed in dark ink.

"Yeah, we saw you sniffing the money and fantasizing about it back there," said Fox Tall. "I'll bet these symbols mean all kinds of things to you!"

"No, I don't think so," said the gorilla.

If I can weigh in at this point, I think the symbols do have meaning. They may not be *loaded* with meaning, it may not be oozing out through the cracks, but I'm sure there's a sliver of meaning.

```
irb> $:
  => ["/usr/lib/ruby/site_ruby/1.8", "/usr/
lib/ruby/site_ruby/1.8/i686-linux",
     "/usr/lib/ruby/site_ruby", "/usr/lib/
ruby/1.8",
     "/usr/lib/ruby/1.8/i686-linux"]
```

Variables which start with the American cash sign are global variables. They can be seen from anywhere in the program, **from inside any scope**. (Dr. Cham used this variable while snooping around The Originals' computer bay.)

So why does the **cash sign followed by a colon** represent an array of **all directories where Ruby will search when you try to load a file with** `require`? The cash sign means "global." But why the colon?

Historically, on many operating systems, a list of directories contains colons which separated each entry. I like to see the colon as a pair of eyes, scanning the directories for files. We store our lookout list behind the eyes.

Here's a few more special global variables:

```
irb> $"        # The $" variable contains all files which
               # have been loaded with `require'
  => ["irb.rb", "e2mmap.rb", "irb/init.rb", ... "rbconfig.rb"]
               # These files are stored somewhere else,
               # but their code is being used
               # in this program.  Much like quoting
               # someone else's work -- these are the
               # footnotes -- hence the double-quote.

irb> $0        # The $0 variable contains the running
               # program's filename.
  => "irb"     # A zero can be considered the beginning
               # of a number count.
               # This variable answers the question,
               # "Where did this program begin?"

irb> $*        # The $* variable contains all the
               # arguments passed into a program.
  => ['--prompt', 'simple']
               # This one is easy to remember, if you
               # remember that Ruby methods also use the
               # asterisk to capture arguments into an array.

# The $! contains the current exception raised.
# The exclamation indicates a state of alarm.  An exception!
irb> begin
irb>   raise TypeError, "I don't believe this information."
irb> rescue
irb>   p $!
irb> end
  => #<TypeError: I don't believe this information.>

# The $@ contains the current backtrace, if an exception was raised.
# The backtrace shows where Ruby was _at_ when the exception fired.
irb> begin
irb>   raise TypeError, "I don't believe this information."
irb> rescue
irb>   p $@
irb> end
```

```
=> ["(irb):25:in `irb_binding'", "/usr/lib/ruby/1.8/irb/
workspace.rb:52:in `irb_binding'", "/usr/lib/ruby/1.8/irb/
workspace.rb:52"]
```

"I don't remember you." Blix looked at the gorilla with great interest. "Are you one of R.K.'s kids or something?"

"Oh, come on!" said Fox Small, holding up a bill with an exclamation mark on it up to the gorilla's nose. "Don't tell me this means *nothing* to you! This one is probably *really important* since it has an exclamation on it. Maybe it pays for emergency stuff! Hospital bills or something!"

"Yeah, surgery!" said Fox Tall.

The gorilla looked at the foxes with disgust from under the brim of his cap. "No, you're wrong. You can't pay for surgeries with that."

"But you see our point," said the small fox. He grabbed some of the other bills. "And you say this bill *cannot* pay for surgeries? Well that sounds like it has a specific *non-surgery-related* purpose. Now, the question mark one. Oh, what would that one be for?"

"Hey, give me those," the gorilla snatched at the bills over the counter, but his long thumb kept getting in the way and every time he thought he had grabbed bills, it turned out he had only grabbed his long thumb.

"Hey, hey, look, he's mad," said Fox Tall, happily clapping. "I wonder why. Did you notice how mad he started getting once we mentioned all these interesting meanings? **We're on to you! We figured out your game so fast!"**

"We totally did!" said Fox Small, one of his elbows caught in the grip of the gorilla, the other arm waving a bill that featured an underscore. "This one's for buying floor supplies, maybe even big rolls of tile and linoleum."

"See," said Fox Tall, working to pry the gorilla's fingers free, "we just have to figure out which is more expensive: surgery or linoleum! This is *so easy!"*

"NO IT'S NOT!" yelled the gorilla, yanking at the smaller fox and battering the fox with his palms. **"YOU DON'T KNOW ANYTHING ABOUT MONKEY MONEY!! YOU DON'T EVEN *HAVE* YOUR OWN KINDS OF MONEY!!"**

"We could *easily* have our own kinds of money!" said Fox Tall, taking the chimp's hat and tossing it to the back of the room, where it sailed behind a wall of safety deposit boxes. "And—*your hat is outta here!*"

"Come on, give him back his bills," said Blix, waving his arms helplessly from the sidelines. "We could really use this guy's help."

"Stop hitting me!" screamed the littlest fox. "I've almost figured out this one with the dots on it!!"

Suddenly, with great precision and without warning, Fox Tall grabbed the monkey's nose and slammed his face down against the counter. The pens and inkpads on its surface rattled and "Bam!" said the fox. The gorilla's eyes spun sleepily as his arms... then his neck... then his head slithered to the floor behind the counter.

Here are a few more global variables you might care to use:

```
irb> $/        # The $/ is the line separator, it is normally set
  => "\n       # to \n, which represents _Enter_
               # or "end of line".  The slash represents a sword
               # slashing lines in a file.


# The line separator controls how methods like each_line
# or readlines breaks up strings.
irb> "Jeff,Jerry,Jill\nMichael,Mary,Myrtle".each_line { |names| p names }
  => "Jeff,Jerry,Jill\n"
  => "Michael,Mary,Myrtle"


# If you change the line separator, you change how many methods work,
# such as each_line. See what happens when I change the line separator
# to a comma.
irb> $/ = ','
irb> "Jeff,Jerry,Jill\nMichael,Mary,Myrtle".each_line { |names| p names }
  => "Jeff,"
  => "Jerry,"
  => "Jill\nMichael,"
  => "Mary,"
  => "Myrtle"
```

```
irb> $,      # The $, variable is the join separator, used when
  => nil     # joining strings with Array#join or Kernel::print.
             # The comma is a common join character.

# The join separator is normally empty.
irb> ['candle', 'soup', 'mackarel'].join
  => "candlesoupmackarel"
irb> $, = ' * '; ['candle', 'soup', 'mackarel'].join
  => "candle * soup * mackarel"

# But, usually, you won't need the global variable.
irb> ['candle', 'soup', 'mackarel'].join ' # '
  => "candle # soup # mackarel"

irb> $;      # The $; variable is the split separator, used when
             # splitting strings
  => nil     # with String#split.

# The split separator is normally empty, which means String#split
# will separate the string where there is whitespace.
irb> "candle  soup\nmackarel".split
  => ["candle", "soup", "mackarel"]
irb> $; = 'a'; "candle  soup\nmackarel".split[10]
  => ["c", "ndle  soup\nm", "ck", "rel"]

# But, usually, you won't need the global variable.
irb> "candle # soup # mackarel".split ' # '
  => ['candle', 'soup', 'mackarel']
```

Outside the *Gorilla Mint*, Blix scolded the foxes. "We could have used that guy's help! If he knows where R.K. is, we could use his cunning!"

"**We don't need that ape's money!**" said Fox Small. "**We can make our *own* money!**"

"**We could support electronic wristbands!**" said Fox Tall.

"His money is worthless," said Blix. "It's gorilla money. It has no value. It's worse than blue crystals."

"But it serves a purpose," said Fox Tall.

---

10 Publisher's note: the reason we didn't edit the original spelling of "mackerel" in this edition.

"No it doesn't," said Fox Small. "He just said it's worthless."

"But what about linoleum and surgeries?" said Fox Tall.

"Yeah," said Fox Small, up at Blix. "What about linoleum and surgeries?"

"If all the hospitals were staffed by gorillas and all the home improvement chains were strictly operated by gorillas, then—YES—you could buy linoleum and surgeries. But I *guarantee* that you would have very sloppy linoleum and very hideous surgeries. I don't think you'd make it out of that economy alive."

"So, if R.K. is so cunning," said Fox Tall, grinning slyly, "why does he print such worthless currency?"

"It's a cover for other activities," said Blix. "Besides, if you're so smart, why did you resort to violently pounding that poor gorilla?"

"I guess that was a bad play," said Fox Tall, hanging his head. "My friend here will tell you that I've been on edge all day."

"And your rage finally reared its fuming snout!" said Fox Small. "You're finally living up to your goatee."

Down the lanes they travelled, the two foxes oblivious to their direction, but having a good time now that they had Blix leading the way with such urgency. They lapsed into a careless wandering right behind Blix and spent their afternoon heckling most of the passersby.

One such target of their ongoing commentary was The Winged Scroll Carriers, pairs of bats that carry documents which need to be immediately sworn and notarized. There can be no delay, they must go swift, there is not even time to roll up the scroll, no, they must drop their swiss cheese and be out the door.

These couriers resemble a kind of Ruby construct called **delimited types**. A long series of characters comprises the scroll, flanked on each side by a bat bracing its curly wings to hold the scroll together. The opening bat wears a hat on which is written **%w**, which identifies the scroll as a set of words.

```
irb> bats = %w{The Winged Scroll Carriers}
  => ['The', 'Winged', 'Scroll', 'Carriers']
```

The **%w** bats and their scroll, when fed into Ruby, emerge as an array of words. This syntax is a shortcut in case you don't want to go through the trouble of decorating each word with commas and quotes. You are in a hurry, too, there can be no delay. You jot out the words between the bats and let Ruby figure out where to cut.

Other bats, other hats. For instance, the **%x** hat runs an external program.

```
irb> %w{ruby --help}
  => ["ruby", "--help"]
irb> %x{ruby --help}
  => "Usage: ruby [switches] [--] [programfile]
[arguments] ..."
```

My favorite is the **%Q** hat, which can also be written as just **%**. This acts just like a double-quoted string, but looks nice when used with strings that run-on for many lines. Like, say you're adding a new method with **eval**.

```
m = "bats!"
eval %(
  def #{ m }
    puts "{" * 100
  end
)
```

Just like a double-quoted string, you can use the string interpolation lilypads inside.

Cloneberries: The More You Eat, The More *You.*

Blixy wagged his head. "Oh, dear me."

"Egads! My hand is pregnant," said Fox Tall, watching the little fox embryo slide about in his palm.

"They are good berries, though," said Blix. "The wine they make from these berries will make ya grow a few eyeballs in your teeth. But no more than that."

"Ah, pain!" yelled Fox Small, as his miniature squeezed out through the pores in his scalp. But soon he was cradling his little self and murmuring lullabies. *Nevermore, nevermore, sweetly sang the nightingale. Winking starlight, sleeping still, whilst perched on a Sycamore stump.*

Making duplicates of Ruby objects is no more than a berry's worth of code.

```
irb> tree = [:berry, :berry, :berry]
  => [:berry, :berry, :berry]
irb> treechild = tree.clone
  => [:berry, :berry, :berry]
```

The **clone** method makes an exact copy of a Ruby object. How does this differ from regular assignment?

```
irb> tree_charles_william_iii = tree
  => [:berry, :berry, :berry]
```

Assigning object to variables only creates more nicknames. The above Array can be called **tree_charles_william_iii** now. Or the shorter **tree**. The same object, but different names.

However, a clone is a copy of an object. You can modify it without affecting the original.

```
irb> treechild << 'flower'
  => [:berry, :berry, :berry, 'flower']
irb> tree
  => [:berry, :berry, :berry]
```

The **clone** method doesn't make copies of everything attached to the object, though. In the array above, only the array is copied, not all the symbols and strings inside.

You may also see the **dup** method used to copy objects. The **dup** method makes copies which aren't as exact. For example, there are objects in Ruby which are "frozen" and can't be altered. If you **clone** the object, you get an exact copy which is also frozen. If you use **dup**, you get an unfrozen copy that you can change if you like.

The **clone** method also copies the metaclass of an object, whereas **dup** does not.

```
irb> o = Object.new
irb> class << o
irb>    def nevermore; :nevermore; end
irb> end

irb> o.clone.nevermore
  => :nevermore
irb> o.dup.nevermore
# NoMethodError: undefined method `nevermore' for
#<Object:0xb7d4a484>
#          from (irb):7
```

You don't always need to make copies of objects, though, since many methods like **collect** and **gsub** and **format** make copies for you as part of their work.

Deer of the Smoky Pink Puffing.

Over the hills and down the valleys, they ran through the grass where the Deer of the Smoky Pink Puffing roam. The sun was obscured by the lumbering pink clouds, emblazoned with deer language, tinting the horizon a gradient of grapefruit and secreting a glow over the meadow. The clouds slid past each other, some bobbing upwards, destined for Canadian relatives. Others landing a readable distance from a recipient's hooves.

"Let's stop! *Please!*" yelled Fox Tall. "You can't expect us to run in this **unbreathable fluff!**"

"Why are you yelling?" said Blix, as a thin stratus telegram wafted behind his legs. "You don't need to raise your voice above a whisper. These long skinny clouds are usually just a mumble or a sigh. They may not even make it all the way."

"All that writing on the cloud is deer talk?" said Fox Small.

"Help! *Where are you guys?*" The taller fox ducked through a stormy tirade comprised of thick, billowing smoke and sharp wisps. He whirled in every direction, "Somebody yell if you're there!"

He searched for a fissure in the dense matter, combing forward with his hands. The verbose, angry clouds responded by prodding him ahead, forcing him into tight corners in their brief pause between sentences. He landed in a sinkhole and kept his head down as the cascades of smoke surged forward.

"Yeah, deer can read this stuff," said Blix. "They just face their target and shoot it out of their nostrils. I once heard of a guy who **rode** a stag's love poem."

"No way," said Fox Small.

"Yep," said Blix. "And that guy was me." Blix reached over his shoulder and latched onto a spiral column of smoke that was twisting just above his head. "You just have to know which clouds are wimpy and which clouds are grandiloquent." Blix let the cloud

Steaks 'n' Slides

My uncles love waterslides and they also love steakhouses.
They have these waterslide days which are directly
followed by a trip over to Joey's Steakhouse. I **hate** Joey's
Steakhouse. It's all big, brown shoe meat. Floppy and
galoshy. Mixed with the stench of the uncles' chlorine.

Pruny fingers on meat slabs is The Revolting.

It's time for steaks and waterslides to come together in a truly
repugnant manner. My uncles have had steaks and waterslides
their whole lives. The dynasty of steaks and waterslides must
come to a close. I will marry them in ways against nature!

Like this:

Hand steaks to riders as they board the waterslide. Rider looks at
the lifeguard. Lifeguard says wait. Rider looks again. The lifeguard
pauses. Then. Okay, it's time. **Go, kid, go!** And the look on that kid's
face as he rushes down the slope, paws full of chuck! **Go, kid, go!**

Kids slide on top of steaks. For safety, we'd
want the slides stacked five steaks deep.

Or, steaks do the sliding. In their own little swim trunks.

Or, people. With steak swim trunks.

People and steaks, side-by-side.

Steaks travelling down waterslides composed of steaks.

Steaks travelling down waterslides made of people.

And, of course, people eating steaks, but their tongues come
out as waterslides and they have to push the steaks up the
waterslides. Which is impossible and a lifeguard has to climb up
the waterslide and manually insert the steak into the esophagus.

Waterslides eating people and steaks eating people.

Waterslides and steaks becoming friends after
smelling people on each other's breath.

Or, steaks befriending waterslides, but waterslides not
reciprocating. Waterslides become increasingly despondent
and detached, getting into bad crowds and sinking into
political extremity. Steaks make ankle bracelets out of people
and leave them in the waterslides' trouser pockets, when the
trousers are unattended. They sneak out of the waterslide
commune via a huge waterslide made of steak swim trunks.

Or, like I said, people with steak swim trunks.

pull him along and when the cloud banked upwards, Blix loosed his grip and kept his feet moving slowly along the ground. "See, here's a good one, long like a broom handle. A guy found one once and it was shaped *exactly* like a car: windshield, driver's side airbag, power steering. Uncanny!"

"*And that guy was—*"

"It was!" And Blix climbed up atop the long icy cloud, with its dangling glyphs, and stood proudly, floating high above the small fox's pointy shadow.

"Oh, I could do that," said Fox Small. "Tall and I go jetskiing all the time. *I've stood up on my jetski.* It's just like that."

Fox Tall dashed through a descending puff, shattering its sentence, which letters came unglued and littered the ground with scrambled words, but he had only succeeded in reaching the depressive portions of the deer correspondence, which manifested itself as a dank and opaque mist.

Meanwhile, his smaller counterpart grabbed a narrow train of smoke that passed under his arm. He was airborned and yelled, **"Tallyho!"** But he held too tightly and the cloud evaporated under his arm and sent him back down with a short hop.

Since you're just beginning your use of Ruby, you may not fully grasp regular expressions (or *regexps*) at first. You may even find yourself clipping out regexps from the Regular Expression Library [11] and pasting them into your code without having the foggiest idea why the expression works. Or *if* it works!

```
loop do
  print "Enter your password: "
  password = gets
  if password.match( /^\w{8,15}$/ )
    break
  else
    puts "** Bad password! Must be 8 to 15 characters!"
  end
end
```

Do you see the unreadable deer language in the example code? The /^\w{8,15}$/ is a regular expression. If I may translate, the regexp is saying, *Please only allow letters, numbers or underscores. No less than eight and no more than fifteen.*

---

[11] http://regexlib.com/DisplayPatterns.aspx

Regular expressions are a mini-language built into Ruby and many other programming languages. I really shouldn't say *mini*, though, since regexps can be twisted and complicated and much more difficult than any Ruby program.

Using regular expressions is extremely simple. It is like the Deer: making the smoke is an arduous process. But hooking your elbow around the smoke and driving it to the Weinerschnitzel to get mustard pretzel dogs is easy.

```
irb> "good_password".match( /^\w{8,15}$/ )
  => #<MatchData:0xb7d54218>
irb> "this_bad_password_too_long".match( /^\w{8,15}$/ )
  => nil
```

The **String#match** method is the *simplest practical use* of regexps. The **match** method checks to see if the string meets the rules inside the regexp. A regexp is only useful with strings, to test strings for a series of conditions. If the conditions are met, a **MatchData** object is returned. If not, you get **nil**.

The most basic regular expressions are for **performing searches** inside strings. Let's say you've got a big file and you want to search it for a word or phrase. Since a bit of time has passed, let's search the Preeventualist's Losing and Finding Registry again.

```
require 'preeventualist'
PreEventualist.searchfound( 'truck' ) do |page|
  page.each_line do |line|
    puts line if line.match( /truck/ )
  end
end
```

This isn't too different from the code we used earlier to search for lines with the word "truck". Earlier we used **puts line if line['truck']**, which is actually a simpler way of searching a string, if you're just looking for a simple word. The regexp **/truck/** is identical. Find the word "truck". Anywhere in the string.

Uhm, what if truck is capitalized. **Truck.** What then?

```
puts line if line.match( /[Tt][Rr][Uu][Cc][Kk]/i )
```

The **character classes** are the sections surrounded by **square brackets**. Each character class gives a list of characters which are valid matches for that spot. (The first spot matches either an uppercase **T** or a lowercase **t**. The second spot matches an **R** or an **r**. And so on.)

But a simpler way to write it is like this:

```
puts line if line.match( /truck/i )
```

The letter **i** modifier at the end of the regexp indicates that the search is **not case-sensitive**. It will match Truck. And TRUCK. And TrUcK. And other ups and downs.

Oh, and maybe you're truck is a certain model number. A T-1000. Or a T-2000. You can't remember. It's a T *something* thousand.

```
puts line if line.match( /T-\d000/ )
```

See, deer language. The **\d** represents a **digit**. It's a place holder in the regexp for any type of number. The regexp will now match T-1000, T-2000, all the way up to T-9000.

CHARACTER CLASSES		
\d	matches digits	can also be written [0-9]
\w	matches word characters (letters, numbers and the underscore)	can also be written [A-Za-z0-9_]
\s	matches whitespace (spaces, tabs, carriage returns, line feeds)	a.k.a. [\t\r\n]
\D	matches everything but digits	a negated set [^\d]
\W	matches everything but word chars	just like [^\w]
\S	matches everything but whitespace	also [^\s]
.	the period matches everything.	

Building a regexp involves chaining these placeholders together to express your search. If you're looking for a number, followed by whitespace: **/\d\s/**. If you're looking for three numbers in a row: **/\d\d\d/**. **The opening and closing slashes mark the beginning and end of the regexp.**

A search for three numbers in a row can also be written as: /\d{3}/. Immediately following a character class like \d, you can use a quantifier symbol to mark how many times you want the character class to be repeated.

QUANTIFIERS		
{n}	match exactly n times	Precisely three numbers in a row is /\d{3}/
{n,}	matches n_ times or _more	Three or more letters in a row is /[a-z]{3,}/i
{n,n2}	matches at least n_ times but no more than _n2 times	So, /[\d,]{3,9}/ matches between three and nine characters which are numbers or commas
*	the asterisk * is short for {0,}	To match a colon, followed by zero or more word characters: /:\w*/
+	the plus is short for {1,}	To match one or more minus or plus signs, use /[-+]+/
?	the question mark is short for {0,1}	To match three numbers followed by an optional period: /\d{3}[.]?/
.	the period matches everything.	

A really common regular expression is for matching phone numbers. American phone numbers (including an area code) can be matched using the digit character class and the precise quantifiers.

```
irb> "Call 909-375-4434" =~ /--/
  => 5
irb> "The number is (909) 375-4434" =~ /[(][)]-/
  => 14
```

This time, instead of using **match** to search for the expression, the =~ operator was used. This operator is the **match operator**, an equals sign followed by **a tilde**. The tilde is like a bit of smoke coming off the edge of a smokestack. Remember the deer, the smoke they blow, a cryptic language just like regular expressions. The smoky tilde points toward the regexp.

The match operator returns a number. The number is the spot in the string where the regular expression matched. So when the match operator returns **5**, it's saying, "Before the match, there are five characters in the string."

If you need to get the full string matched, you can use the special **$&** global variable if you're using the match operator. Or, if you're using the **match** method, you can get the full string by converting the **MatchData** object to a string.

```
# Using =~ and $& together.
irb> "The number is (909) 375-4434" =~ /[(]\d{3}[)]\s*\
d{3}-\d{4}/
  => 14
irb> $&
  => "(909) 375-4434"


# Using the MatchData object.
irb> phone = /[(]\d{3}[)]\s*\d{3}-\d{4}/.match("The number
is (909) 375-4434")
  => #<MatchData:0xb7d51680>
  => # irb> phone.to_s
  => "(909) 375-4434"
```

Most Rubyists prefer the second approach, as it uses an object within a *local variable* rather than a *global variable*. Global variables are kind of sketchy, since they can be easily overwritten. If you run two regular expressions in a row, the global variable gets overwritten the second time. But with local variables, you can keep both matches around as long as the variables are named differently.

Other than matching, another common use of regular expression is to do **search-and-replace** from within Ruby. You can search for the word "cat" and replace it with the word "banjo." Sure, you can do that with strings or regexps.

```
irb> song = "I swiped your cat / And I stole your cathodes"
irb> song.gsub 'cat', 'banjo'
  => "I swiped your banjo / And I stole your banjohodes"


irb> song.gsub /\bcat\b/, 'banjo'
  => "I swiped your banjo / And I stole your cathodes"
```

The **gsub** method is named for "global substitution." Notice how in the first example it replaced the word "cat" and the first three letters of "cathodes." Strings also have a simple **sub** method which will substitute only once.

And so this chapter ends, with Blix and the Foxes cruising aloft the solid pink belched from a very outspoken deer somewhere in those pastures.

6. Just Stopping To Assure You That the Porcupine Hasn't Budged

The porcupine and his kite again.

7. I'm Out

Quil uses a banjo as an umbrella.

One day, back around the time I met Bigelow (that dog who walked off with the balloons), I came back to my apartment hauling some board games I'd bought at a garage sale. And Quil was on my porch. Which stunned me since she'd been in San Antonio for like three years. She was sleeping in a sleeping bag on my porch.

She had run out of money to go to art school, so she stayed at my place for five months or so.

I found this used bunkbed for our place. At night

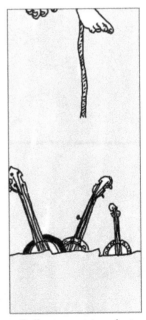

Quil escapes to a hot air balloon, an act the banjos champion.

we'd sit in our beds and read each other stories from our notebooks. I was writing a book about a kid who's a detective and he's trying to figure out who killed this kid on his tennis team and all these animals end up helping him figure it out. She was writing a book about this kid who puts an ad in the classifieds to get other kids to join his made-up cult and they end up building a rocket ship. But during most of her book these kids are lost in the woods and pretty directionless, which I got a kick out of hearing each night.

Yeah, each night it was poetry or stories or ideas for tricking our neighbors. Our neighbor Justin was a big fan of Warhammer and he had all these real swords and tunics. We decided to make suits of armor out of tin foil and go attack his apartment. We started ransacking his apartment and he loved it. So he made his own suit of armor out of tin foil and we all went to a professional glamour studio and had a quality group shot taken.

Four Quils feast on the carcasses
of jackals.

I'm not saying my life is any better than yours. I just miss my sister. Life isn't like that now. We're dissolved or something.

I don't know. I'm confused. Is this growing up? Watching all your feathers come off? And even though some of those feathers were the most lovely things?

I'm having a hard time telling who stopped it all up. Who stopped loving who? Did I stop caring? Maybe I only saw her in two-dimensions and I didn't care to look at the other angles. I only saw planes. Then she shimmied up the z-axis when I wasn't looking and I never did the homework to trace the coordinates. A limb on a geometrical tree and I am insisting on circles.

Blix was right. I'm in no shape to write this book. Goodbye until I can shake this.

When You Wish Upon a Beard

Okayyy... so he doesn't talk?

No. But check out this new guy we invented!

A A

Hi.

So here's about the [SEND] method.

```
>> "bacon".send :size
=> 5
        —AND ALSO—
>> "bacon".send "size"
=> 5
```

since "bacon".size itself equals 5.

Such preparation!

Okay. Watch how it works.

Like, imagine an adventure.
```
print "Banquet Room. Do what?"
what_to_do = gets.strip
```
The banquet room is an object, right??
```
class BanquetRoom
    def look; "Red with mirrors" end
    def stab; "The room screams!" end
    def sleep; "Ahh, you slept on food" end
end
Room = BanquetRoom.new
```
Now, you've got the what_to_do, so let's use it.
```
Room.send what_to_do
```
This could also be written:
```
eval("Room.#{what_to_do}")
```
But that is SOOOO unpredictable!

*the 'strip' removes spaces from beginning and end.

WELL, I'm off!

BYE!

that was cool! :send!!

we love you!

my chapter.

---

1 Publisher's note: Chapter 8, Heaven's Harp, is blank in the Wayback Machine version and missing from https://poignant.guide.

About this Edition

This edition of *Why's (Poignant) Guide to Ruby* was brought to life for Brighton Ruby 2020. Here are some notes about how we went about it.

The publisher, typesetter and designer of this edition is Consonance, a team of publishers[1] who are also web developers[2] of a Rails app[3] that book publishers use to run their businesses. We are also vocal advocates for technical literacy in book publishing[4].

Being both publishers and programmers means we are uniquely placed to produce a new paperback edition of this seminal work. So when Andy Croll[5], organiser of the Brighton Ruby conference[6], wondered aloud (via email) to me, Emma Barnes (Consonance's CEO), whether gifting a print edition of the book to his attendees at the Brighton Ruby 2020 event would be possible, we were excited to help.

---

1 https://snowbooks.com and https://makeourbook.com
2 "Corporate" site can be found at https://generalproducts.co
3 https://consonance.app
4 Through initiatives such as https://dayofcode.co.uk and
   https://sideprojectsummer.com
5 https://andycroll.com/
6 https://brightonruby.com/

The project

We came to various decisions about layout, design, and printing-in-the-age-of-pandemic in Basecamp, which I thought was rather poetic, being the app written in Ruby that spun off Rails, the framework that brought Ruby to the masses.

The files

Retrieving the original files was fairly straightforward because someone had done all the work already. We cloned their repo[7], and converted its Markdown files to the ICML Adobe InDesign proprietary format, using Pandoc.

The grid

My sharp-eyed General Products colleague Andy Pearson[8] and I created the grid for the book, using much the same approach as we'd use for a website grid. The use of whitespace, columns and baselines to good effect unifies web and print disciplines.

7 At https://github.com/mislav/poignant-guide
8 https://andypearson.co

The code

The code in the original Markdown got smooshed into a syntax highlighting mess between Rouge tags that InDesign couldn't handle:

```
{% highlight %} marked-up text {% end %}
```

So formatting the code in the book required more drastic intervention. And we were constrained on colour. So I created a new VSCode monochrome theme, based on the useful starting point i Light[9]. Then:

- I copied each individual bit of code from the original HTML in the browser...

- pasted into VSCode in my new monochrome theme...

- copied from that into Google Docs, of all things...

- so I could export to .docx which was the only format I found persisted the local character formatting (italics, underline etc)...

- and copied and pasted each individual bit of code to the right place in InDesign...

- and then in InDesign I used "find by format" to replace locally-formatted italics, bold and underlines with character styles for consistency and to avoid the local styles being overwritten by paragraph styles.

I guess the programming parallel for that murky bit of typesetting workflow is "sometimes you have to deal with legacy data". Next time, LaTeX?

The editing

Our editorial principle was to adhere to Why's original intent as much as possible. We also wanted to make the type large enough to be pleasantly readable, so sometimes we chose to allow lines of code to wrap, or break, in different places than in the original. We corrected a number of typos, and made some edits including those made on the maintained fork of the

---

9 https://github.com/ctrlplusb/i-theme, a fork of https://github.com/arthurwhite/white-theme-vscode

site. But on the whole the book remains true to its original format, including the original spacing in the code where possible. We even reused Georgia as the body font.

The format

We toyed with the idea of a mass-market paperback format, to make the book pocket-sized and to fit nicely on shelves alongside thrillers and the like. And the code and the images fitted our initial layouts. But using the tried-and-tested mock-up technique of actually printing out a couple of pages, jamming them into an old Terry Pratchett paperback and seeing how they felt showed us that the format was too tight:

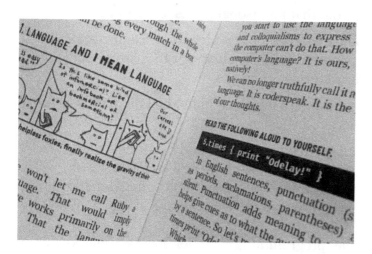

It's the equivalent of tests passing, but with a rubbish user experience. So we went for a bigger format.

The rest of the book

There are a lot of other things that go into making a book. As with programming, non-typesetters and non-cover-designers wouldn't believe how much needs to be done to build a robust, maintainable layout. In particular, many paragraphs needed styles adding manually to avoid widows and orphans, and sidebars needed laying out within the flow of the text even though they spanned many pages. Foxes were redrawn in Illustrator. Image alts were made into captions. Art was faithfully redrawn by hand and scanned. Locked-down children were enlisted to proofread and check that the right foxes were on the right pages.

The effort

The layout of this book was non-trivial, and it occured at a strange time, as we were slipping into pandemic lockdown in the UK, with all the health, financial, social, family and general apocalyptic issues it brought. But Ruby is important to us and to so many people, and making this book felt like a good use of whatever mental energy we had: to honour and celebrate something that played such a memorable role in our individual Ruby journeys.

We also wanted to do anything we could to support Brighton Ruby, which has long been a fantastic way of nuturing the Ruby community. And as the Brighton Ruby conference succumbed to the need to cancel, a physical object, posted to the delegates, seemed even more important as a way to unite the community in socially-distant times.

A message for Why

If Why ever gets his hands on a copy of this book and reads this far: thank you for all you did for so many of us. You cemented in our minds the notion that Ruby is special. And you're very funny. It's interesting that you chose the medium of a long-form book to broadcast your message. Books, like Ruby, have grace and nuance. They have narrative arcs, beauty in their expression, and flow. Writing can be poetic, terse, elegant, descriptive—all the reasons why we love Ruby. Your ode to the language influenced us all, and is part of what makes us proud to be Rubyists. We appreciate your effort, and hope you approve of this edition.

A message from FreeAgent

Here at FreeAgent we're a friendly bunch, making small businesses happier and more successful by putting them in control of their finances.

Our award-winning online accounting software is designed specifically for freelancers, small businesses and their accountants. Around 100,000 customers currently use FreeAgent to manage their business accounts and day-to-day bookkeeping.

At FreeAgent everyone has the opportunity to shape and influence where the company is going. Open planning sessions keep everyone up to date on our strategic objectives and weekly Town Hall meetings ensure that everyone knows what's going on across the team.

We work hard to make FreeAgent a great place to work and to ensure that everyone feels at home. We also provide a comprehensive package of employee benefits, which are carefully selected to protect our team, promote a healthy lifestyle, and provide peace of mind.

Keep an eye on freeagent.com/careers for upcoming opportunities to join the team.

A message from Cookpad

Cookpad is happy to help support Brighton Ruby for the 5th year running!

Our mission is to make everyday cooking fun, and as the world's largest recipe sharing community, with over 100 million monthly average users, we also want to make everyday *coding* fun. This is why we rely on Ruby at the heart of our tech stack.

The choices we make shape our world, and when we cook, the choices we make have an impact on ourselves, the people we love, the growers and producers we buy from, and the environment we live in. By solving issues related to everyday cooking and helping more people to cook, we believe we can help build a better world.

Learn more at
https://www.cookpadteam.com

www.ingramcontent.com/pod-product-compliance
Lightning Source LLC
Chambersburg PA
CBHW031237050326
40690CB00007B/835